DIRTY STORY

BY JOHN PATRICK SHANLEY

★

★

DRAMATISTS
PLAY SERVICE
INC.

DIRTY STORY
Copyright © 2003, John Patrick Shanley

All Rights Reserved

SPECIAL NOTE

SPECIAL NOTE ON SONGS AND RECORDINGS

*This play is dedicated to Prof. Terence Patrick Moran,
a tremendous enemy of bullshit.*

DIRTY STORY was originally produced by the LAByrinth Theater Company (Robin Kramer and John Gould Rubin, Producers; Stephanie Yankwitt, Associate Producer) in New York City, opening on February 18, 2003. It was directed by John Patrick Shanley; the set design was by Michelle Malavet; the lighting design was by Jeremy Morris; the sound design was by Elizabeth Rhodes; the costume design was by Mimi O'Donnell; and the stage manager was Mary E. Leach. The cast was as follows:

BRUTUS .... David Deblinger
WANDA .... Florencia Lozano
FRANK .... Chris McGarry
LAWRENCE/WATSON .... Michael Puzzo

CHARACTERS

BRUTUS
WANDA
FRANK
LAWRENCE/WATSON

PLACE

A park.

TIME

The present.

DIRTY STORY

ACT ONE

Scene 1

Music. A park. Two outdoor chess tables. A trash can. A little bench, Center. Brutus is drinking coffee, playing a game of chess alone. Across the way, another man, an aging English patrician, Lawrence, also plays chess alone; he's listening to music on a headset. Lawrence raises a sign which reads: FICTION. He lowers it. The music segues into street sounds. Wanda enters. She's pulling a six-foot palm tree in a luggage carrier. She approaches Lawrence.

WANDA. Mister Chiappa? Brutus Chiappa?
LAWRENCE. I don't even want to be here.
WANDA. I'm sure you don't.
LAWRENCE. I just want to go home.
WANDA. I'm sure you do. But are you … (Brutus Chiappa)?
LAWRENCE. *(Overlapping.)* Please! I just want to go home to my chair, my dog, and my mother!
WANDA. You're not Brutus Chiappa, are you?
LAWRENCE. No.
BRUTUS. Are you Wanda?
WANDA. Yes?
BRUTUS. I think you want me. I'm Brutus.
WANDA. Oh. Hi. I'm Wanda. *(To Lawrence.)* Sorry.
LAWRENCE. I just want to go home. And I'm going to go home

in a little bit.

BRUTUS. Never mind him. He has nothing to do with anything.

WANDA. Brutus?

BRUTUS. Yes.

WANDA. Oh, I'm sorry. There's no picture on your book jackets.

BRUTUS. It's not worthy of further explanation.

WANDA. Nice to meet you.

BRUTUS. You have a large plant.

WANDA. Yeah, good buy on Sixth Avenue. It's all the real estate I can afford. Am I interrupting something?

BRUTUS. Nothing to be done about it.

WANDA. I could come back.

BRUTUS. That's ridiculous.

WANDA. I just noticed you're playing a game of chess.

BRUTUS. Yeah.

WANDA. *(Re: Lawrence.)* He is, too.

BRUTUS. I don't know that man. We just happen to be sharing a public space.

WANDA. Is it something people do now? Play chess alone? In proximity to other people playing chess alone?

BRUTUS. I don't know what people do. I can only speak for myself. I like to play alone.

WANDA. It seems funny. I mean two people who want to play chess so close by each other. Seems silly they're not in the same game.

BRUTUS. Simply because two people are physically near each other doesn't mean they should be friends.

WANDA. Chess isn't about friendship, it's about combat.

BRUTUS. Even conflict requires common ground. Come on, sit down. I don't like to look up at people.

WANDA. Oh, of course. I'm sorry. Thank you. *(She sits.)* I have been deeply affected by your poetry, your essays, your books for a long time now. Thank you for agreeing to meet with me.

BRUTUS. I don't mind meeting. I'll go to meetings. I'm willing to meet with anybody. Have you heard different or something?

WANDA. No. I just want to acknowledge that it's an act of generosity to take the time to give a graduate student the benefit of your experience.

BRUTUS. *(Rummages in a valise.)* You seem a little old to be a graduate student. I was out of graduate school and established in the world by the time I was ... How old are you?

WANDA. I'm still quite young. *(He pulls a manuscript out of his bag, gets up with his coffee.)*

BRUTUS. By the time I was twenty-six. Here. *(He's handed her the manuscript and heads for the trash can.)*

WANDA. For some of us, being a student is a lifelong occupation.

BRUTUS. I have a nephew like that. His parents are suicidal. *(He throws his coffee lid in the trash.)*

WANDA. I didn't mean I don't work. I pay my way.

BRUTUS. You don't get a little scholarship money or something? A little subsidy?

WANDA. Some. It's based on merit.

BRUTUS. You're a tomboy.

WANDA. What?

BRUTUS. All right, all right. I read your ... What do you call it? A homily? *(He sits on the bench.)*

WANDA. A novel. *(He pours his coffee into the palm tree. She reacts.)*

BRUTUS. It was wretched, it was ignominious, it was a shonda. I lament that you wrote it. It takes seventeen trees to make one ton of paper. You might think about that the next time you consider writing.

WANDA. Oh, I'm sorry if it wasn't good.

BRUTUS. It wasn't good.

WANDA. Could you clarify in what way it wasn't good? *(He gets up.)*

BRUTUS. Don't you read the paper? Hasn't anybody told you the news?

WANDA. What?

BRUTUS. Fiction is dead. *(He tosses his empty cup in the trash.)*

WANDA. You don't really believe that.

BRUTUS. Fiction is a fabrication. A lie. An unfounded fantasy. We're not interested anymore. We don't care. We don't want to suspend our disbelief. Fiction is dead.

WANDA. But then what's alive?

BRUTUS. Nonfiction.

WANDA. All fiction is dead and all nonfiction without limitation is alive?

BRUTUS. Correct. But all nonfiction is not of interest. One

wishes to be in some sense surprised. The pages should set off a border skirmish. "I knew that but I didn't know I knew it." That kind of thing. *(Brutus has wandered over to Lawrence's game and stolen a peek. Lawrence covers his game, exclaiming:)*

LAWRENCE. Oh no you don't! *(Brutus does an answering gesture.)*

BRUTUS. Oh yes I do! *(Swings back to his table and seat.)* We want work which is both credible AND fantastic. In short, it should smack of accuracy, but fall short or long of agreed-upon truth. Like plausible gossip.

WANDA. I've always thought of gossip as a social evil.

BRUTUS. It holds a potent fascination.

WANDA. For the mob.

BRUTUS. Sometimes the mob is on to something.

WANDA. What about your book *Understanding Japanese*?

BRUTUS. What about it?

WANDA. That was nonfiction. Is that an example of this unagreed-upon truth?

BRUTUS. Doesn't interest me anymore.

WANDA. Why not?

BRUTUS. I was writing about fashion in Japan acting as a substitute for rage. The Eastern idea of face recast as the Western idea of the individual. Unfortunately, the subject matter, by definition, confined me to appearances.

WANDA. It was a wonderful book.

BRUTUS. I'm through with it! And I'm through with the Japanese!

WANDA. May I ask why?

BRUTUS. Their last great idea was the kamikaze.

WANDA. That's offensive.

BRUTUS. The truth usually is. Modern Japan is Karaoke.

WANDA. You like to provoke.

BRUTUS. I like to poke open assumptions and let the stink out.

WANDA. But if your book wasn't nonfiction, what was it? Sort of an essay?

BRUTUS. An essay? Look. Your novel is no good.

WANDA. *(Explodes.)* GOD *(Controls.)* dammit! You poured coffee into my tree!

BRUTUS. Yes. Your book is one of those utopian fantasies founded on an insanely optimistic view of human beings.

WANDA. Don't you think we should aim high?

BRUTUS. Not if you want to hit something.

WANDA. But what if I want to envision something new, something that doesn't exist, and by describing it, set in motion its genesis?

BRUTUS. Like Karl Marx?

WANDA. In a way.

WATSON. Karl Marx.

BRUTUS. Oh ho, you woke him up. Look at that. Another English Lefty. Probably thinks Joe Stalin was a boy scout. *(To Lawrence.)* You ever hear of the Gulag, you hamhock!?

LAWRENCE. Absolutely! No humidity. *(Brutus looks from Lawrence to Wanda like: Am I alone here?)*

WANDA. You can't fool me. I know you have ideals. What about your books of poetry?

BRUTUS. I've sworn off. There's a reason the poet's instrument is the lyre.

WANDA. The ideal is important. There's a mindless momentum that comes out of the past. The counteracting force is idealism. I wrote this book to change the course of things.

BRUTUS. Too bad it doesn't have a plot.

WANDA. No, it doesn't have a plot. It IS a plot, the blueprint for a dream. At one time, a man imagined the Taj Mahal, then people built it, now it exists. That's what I want to do.

BRUTUS. You've let your imagination pollute your aesthetic.

WANDA. Imagination is the future's workshop.

BRUTUS. Listen to me. Never write a book like this again. Confine yourself to nonfiction. Better yet, restrict yourself to reading. Your manuscript has no understanding of the possible, much less the real. Furthermore, it's a gloss on a gloss. An utterly unoriginal, very long What If? You want me to sloganize it for you? It's all sugar and no shit.

WANDA. You don't have to be vulgar.

BRUTUS. *(Makes a smoothing gesture.)* How do you know?

WANDA. Restless?

BRUTUS. Always.

WANDA. I can fix the book.

BRUTUS. You can burn the book.

11

WANDA. There's a real need behind this work! Maybe I haven't found the right words yet, but they exist in my heart and I will find a way to say them!

BRUTUS. Big feelings are not the same as big ideas.

WANDA. Display some doubt, would you? You would benefit from exhibiting some doubt.

BRUTUS. Really? I don't think so. I suggest you go home.

WANDA. I'll never give up.

BRUTUS. Go home, chickadee.

WANDA. I will be heard.

BRUTUS. Wipe the spittle off your face, take up a new hobby.

WANDA. No.

BRUTUS. No one wants to hear from you what should happen in life. How they should live. You do not have a better idea. This book is dead.

WANDA. Then I'll write another one. Don't you understand? I don't care about the book. I care about the thing behind it.

BRUTUS. And what's that?

WANDA. Me! There has to be a place for me! In life. Where I can speak and where I am heard. And I believe there are people who want to hear what I have to say. Even if you're not one of them. Even if I don't know what it is that I have to say yet. So maybe you're right on this one, okay? Let's say you're absolutely right. This book is a piece of shit. If that's the case, *(Throws it in trash can.)* it's chucked.

BRUTUS. You've managed to surprise me. This is how you respond to a destructive critic? Are you a masochist?

WANDA. I want to improve myself and I'm willing to pay the price.

BRUTUS. What are you, German?

WANDA. I, well, it's … Actually, I am German, of German descent, on both sides. How did you know that?

BRUTUS. I was joking. But obviously humor has less wit than blood. I would've thought you were a Jew.

WANDA. No one thinks I'm a Jew. I am a Jew.

BRUTUS. A German Jew.

WANDA. What are you?

BRUTUS. I'm a Jew German. So why did you make this 348-page mud pie?

WANDA. I think of it as a folktale.

BRUTUS. Folktales beguile.

WANDA. Why did you agree to meet me if you thought so little of it?

BRUTUS. I had to get out of the house. My work drives me mad.

WANDA. But there must've been something in it that you thought valuable in some small way?

BRUTUS. I liked one word in your cover letter.

WANDA. What was it?

BRUTUS. "Damsel." You used the word "damsel."

WANDA. I was actually ashamed that I used that word. I thought it was a bit coy.

BRUTUS. Coy as in "charm"? You were trying to charm me?

WANDA. Well, yes.

BRUTUS. Looking over your fan like some crafty contessa? Dropping your handkerchief. Using this medieval word and this oblique tone to get what you wanted.

WANDA. That's right.

BRUTUS. Which is what?

WANDA. I was trying to arouse your chivalry. So you would want to help me.

BRUTUS. My chivalry. So you're a romantic.

WANDA. Somewhat.

BRUTUS. A perilous, perilous thing to be. *(She turns to steel for a moment.)*

WANDA. It has power, too. *(A pause.)*

LAWRENCE. Excuse me.

WANDA. Yes? *(Brutus grabs her wrist to hold her attention. She looks at his hand on her wrist.)*

BRUTUS. And has this use of medieval mythology worked for you in the past?

WANDA. No, actually, it never has.

BRUTUS. So that's why you were ashamed you used the word "damsel" in your letter. You were mortified to be using a ploy which had already proved itself a bust. It's like you never learn.

WANDA. *(Removes his hand.)* But I do learn. *(A pause.)*

LAWRENCE. Excuse me.

WANDA. Yes?

LAWRENCE. Do you have the time?

BRUTUS. It's twelve o'clock.

LAWRENCE. I'll be leaving soon.

BRUTUS. I can't wait.

LAWRENCE. You'll miss me when I'm gone.

BRUTUS. I doubt that.

WANDA. You say you don't know that man?

BRUTUS. That's right. He's just some misplaced duffer, one of those types that show up in the park and like to oversee everything. *(Calls to Lawrence.)* Right, Pop?

LAWRENCE. *(Indicating his headset.)* Mozart.

WANDA. I think you're just testy because ... Are you working on something now that's frustrating?

BRUTUS. Your blue jeans make me laugh.

WANDA. Why?

BRUTUS. The intelligensia attempting to identify with the worker. Chairman Mao couture. A vestige of the '60s. But you want service, don't you?

WANDA. Have you looked at this theory that we're all descended from seven mothers?

BRUTUS. I'm aware of it.

WANDA. What do you think?

BRUTUS. I think the man who formulated that theory was a eunuch.

WANDA. Oh, come on. He was a scientist propounding a scientific idea.

BRUTUS. The idea that we're all descended from seven mothers is not a scientific idea. It's a political idea.

WANDA. And you don't like the politics.

BRUTUS. I don't like politics masquerading as science any more than I care for aggression disguised as dialogue.

WANDA. What are you talking about?

BRUTUS. You.

WANDA. Me?

BRUTUS. Seven mothers. You're interfering with my work. *(He starts gathering up his chess pieces.)*

WANDA. How?

BRUTUS. This is why I need isolation.

WANDA. I would think an informed exchange could only be useful.

BRUTUS. You don't understand who you're dealing with.

WANDA. You said your work was driving you mad.

BRUTUS. It is. *(Stops collecting his chess pieces.)* I'm chasing an idea, but it runs from me like a truant.

WANDA. What's the idea?

BRUTUS. Story.

WANDA. Story?

BRUTUS. *(Gestures and gestures again, as he speaks, as if smoothing down chaos or casting a spell.)* Storytelling as a force. Storytelling as an invasive, itinerant, organizing principle. Like the Roman army. Story invades experience, reshapes it into its own cultural likeness, and then moves on. Another analogy. This one agricultural. Cotton farming. Storytelling is like cotton farming. A voracious crop that depletes the soil. It uses up one field after another. Poetry. Drama. The novel. The movie. Each medium exploited to the point of exhaustion, and then dropped. My question: When will this story-telling impulse stop eroding forms and itself become bankrupt? Is that happening now? If so, what follows? And perhaps most impor-tantly, what will be the effect on the biggest story of all? History. If Story abandons History, will we come to imagine History in other terms? Or is History, as the Germans so recently declared, dead?

WANDA. Wow. Ambitious stuff.

BRUTUS. By "ambitious," do you mean grandiose?

WANDA. Not in a pejorative sense.

BRUTUS. That's the umbrella idea. You can't address all of any umbrella at once. You've got to go spoke by spoke. I'm thinking smaller at the moment. An illustration. Something which pertains.

WANDA. What?

BRUTUS. Melodrama. *(Lawrence stands abruptly, sweeps his pieces into a box.)*

LAWRENCE. Melodrama! Melodrama! Is that painted whore out about swishing her scarlet skirt again? Not on my watch. I've had a bellyful of that wench. You're on your own. Goodbye. *(He exits.)*

WANDA. I guess he's not a fan of melodrama. *(Brutus crosses to Lawrence's table and starts to unpack his chess pieces, setting up Lawrence's endgame.)*

BRUTUS. He just likes to slip on his own bar of soap.

WANDA. What are you doing?

15

BRUTUS. He was at my table.

WANDA. Oh. So you're interested in the storytelling impulse as manifested in melodrama?

BRUTUS. Yes.

WANDA. What do you mean by "melodrama" exactly? You mean like soap opera?

BRUTUS. No, not like soap opera. Soap opera is a late unrobust example of what I mean. A better model would be the serial. *The Perils of Pauline.*

WANDA. Wasn't that a movie?

BRUTUS. Early silent film. 1914. Girl tied to the railroad tracks by a villain. Train coming. It contains the archetypes I need. The Villain and the Victim.

WANDA. So it's sort of raw, unsophisticated ...

BRUTUS. Popular. Exactly.

WANDA. I wouldn't think that would interest you. It's so ... unrooted.

BRUTUS. No, your work is unrooted. *The Perils of Pauline* is rooted.

WANDA. In what?

BRUTUS. Originally, human behavior. Now, human mythology. Even genetic memory.

WANDA. So she's tied to the tracks by this villain, the train is coming. And what happens then?

BRUTUS. I don't care about the rest of it.

WANDA. But what happens?

BRUTUS. She's saved.

WANDA. By who?

BRUTUS. A cowboy or something. Cuts her loose, kills the Villain or something.

WANDA. So there's a hero.

BRUTUS. Not interested in a hero.

WANDA. But isn't the hero an archetype, too? The Villain, the Victim, and the Hero.

BRUTUS. In my view, the hero is only an interruption. For my purposes, there is no hero.

WANDA. But then won't she just get squashed by the train?

BRUTUS. Is that what you think happens?

WANDA. Not necessarily, I suppose. I think, if you were to look at it as a fairy tale, it might be about a change in perception. The male figure, initially viewed by the woman as a threat, transforms into a positive figure as a result of emotional crisis. The train.

BRUTUS. There are two people in this story. Everything isn't an extension of your ego.

WANDA. I know that.

BRUTUS. All problems aren't solved by negotiating with yourself.

WANDA. I didn't say they were.

BRUTUS. Obviously, you've never been married.

WANDA. But actually, I have.

BRUTUS. I trust it did not end well.

WANDA. No, it didn't.

BRUTUS. Men aren't dreams that women have. There weren't seven mothers and no fathers. Men exist separately from your need for them. We aren't lessons for you to learn. We aren't mistakes you make or don't make. We are worlds, we are countries, and we have our ways.

WANDA. I'm aware that you exist.

BRUTUS. As I relate to you.

WANDA. Exclusive of me.

BRUTUS. Why did you send me that awful book?

WANDA. I didn't know it was awful. Do you really mean that you agreed to meet me on the basis of one word in my COVER LETTER?

BRUTUS. Yes.

WANDA. And that word was "damsel"?

BRUTUS. "Damsel" is a melodramatic icon.

WANDA. Are you somewhat nuts?

BRUTUS. Only to the frogs, my dear. Are you a frog? Do you want to have ideas that legitimately unspool from within? Or are you content to sit on your lilypad believing that you are having thoughts when what you are actually having are belches caused by swallowing undigested chunks of culture?! Originality is not for frogs croaking in chorus. I'll tell you something real. Originality is soul. Every era has its words. There's a word around these days. Authenticity. People are looking for authenticity. It's just the latest word. People are looking for their souls. They climb mountains looking for it, go into the desert, mingle with the destitute. Enter tombs. You think I'm crazy? You've just joined the villagers chasing Dr. Frankenstein's monster up the hill. There was a movie! And no one understood it. Those villagers were the Nazis. And what was the Creature? The Creature was Soul. "It's monstrous! Kill it!" Maybe they were right. But they started a fire in the castle that's burning still. That's it. I've gotta go.

WANDA. But the monster killed a little girl!

BRUTUS. Is that what you think happened?

WANDA. Isn't it?

BRUTUS. I've got to go.

WANDA. But we've just started talking!

BRUTUS. I have to get back to my writing. I haven't written a word all day. I realize in talking to you, I am squandering something that could be part of my work. I can't afford to talk anymore.

WANDA. Please! This always happens to me.

BRUTUS. What?

WANDA. Everyone wants to get away from me. Nobody likes me. It's the story of my life.

BRUTUS. Do you think I'm popular?

WANDA. Compared to me, yes.

BRUTUS. I doubt that. *(She rushes to the trash can, retrieves her manuscript.)*

WANDA. I want to understand why my book is bad.

BRUTUS. Look in the mirror. Goodbye.

WANDA. I'll call you.

BRUTUS. Don't.

WANDA. Thank you for talking to me.

BRUTUS. Only a German Jew could say that. *(He grabs her manuscript and throws it on the ground. He goes. Music. She starts to pick up the scattered pages. The scene change takes place around her. She clutches the pages to her bosom, then makes a decision, and throws it in the trash. Makes a balletic move to express her frustration and longing. Circles her palm tree like a ballerina, rolls it downstage, looks through its fronds as if a sad jungle girl. Then tips it onto her back, and slowly walks off. As ...)*

Scene 2

... Brutus enters his apartment with a glass of wine and opens one of the three large shuttered windows. Behind the shutter, the sash is open. The music continues. It's a loft space. An old metal ladder, an old movie light on wheels. A metal wardrobe, a sawhorse, lumber. A table set for two. A daisy in a small vase. A salad and a bottle of olive oil. Brutus is wearing tight-fitting pants and boots, a white shirt. Wanda enters wearing jeans, a T-shirt and carrying her own glass of wine. The music segues into heavy truck sounds. Brutus shuts the window. The outside noise stops abruptly. A socially tense atmosphere.

BRUTUS. When I moved here, this area was a wasteland. Actually, it still is. But now it has pretensions. I tore out all the closets years ago. I like to see my belongings around me. I move my bed almost every day. This table was over by the window this morning. I have everything on wheels. *(Moves a side table a couple of feet during the next line, does that smoothing gesture.)* I'm addicted to a feeling of impermanence.

WANDA. Restless.

BRUTUS. Yes.

WANDA. That's so funny.

BRUTUS. How so?

WANDA. I'm the opposite. I've had all this impermanence and all I dream of is of settling down and having a home. What a great space!

BRUTUS. You've got to be kidding.

WANDA. No. It has a romantic pentimento.

BRUTUS. It's a rathole. Precious to me, yes. Though make me a better offer and I'd vacate like a shot. But I don't see that happening. No. This is it. This is the last stop. Awful.

WANDA. Wouldn't you like to have something green?

BRUTUS. Then I'd have to water it. I don't want to take that on. Danka shen for the daisy.

WANDA. You're welcome. It's become very swank, this part of town.

BRUTUS. I know. Who would've guessed that saying you live in the Meat District would be appealing?

WANDA. No, there's something about it.

BRUTUS. You come up against yourself here. To that much I can attest.

WANDA. You get morose, don't you?

BRUTUS. I brood.

WANDA. This salad is wonderful!

BRUTUS. It's the olive oil. I have very good olive oil.

WANDA. Where do you get it?

BRUTUS. My parents. See? Chiappa. The family business.

WANDA. You have olive groves? *(He gets up abruptly with his dish. Puts it on the side table.)*

BRUTUS. I don't. It's an old story. Family's wealthy, I'm not. *(He snatches her plate, though she's still eating, puts it on the side table, and rolls the lot to an offstage kitchen.)*

WANDA. But you must do well with your writing. *(Brutus exits, speaking from Off.)*

BRUTUS. *(O.S.)* I'm broke. I used to make money. I have a body of work. But royalties peter away if there's nothing new to excite the public. *(Reenters.)* And there's the problem. I can't write anything new. *(He's headed for the open shutter.)*

WANDA. What about that idea you were telling me?

BRUTUS. I can't write it. I'll think it, but I can't write it down.

WANDA. Why not? *(He looks out the window.)*

BRUTUS. I stare out the window when I should be working. I can't tear my eyes away from the spectacle of the world passing me by.

WANDA. What do you think about when you're doing that?

BRUTUS. My parents. What they want me to do. *(He shuts the shutter. He gestures that he doesn't want to continue in this vein.)*

WANDA. Speaking of the past, do you want to hear something really weird?

BRUTUS. Sure.

WANDA. My grandfather lived here.

BRUTUS. What do you mean?

WANDA. I was talking to my Aunt Zelda this morning, she saw

your address. This was the first place my grandfather lived in this country.

BRUTUS. Coincidence. The refuge of the unimaginative conversationalist!

WANDA. Why do you do that? *(He's uncomfortable. He gets up.)*

BRUTUS. So you were married?

WANDA. Yes.

BRUTUS. Were you in love?

WANDA. I thought so. *(He grabs up some used silverware off the table, exits to the offstage kitchen, leaving her alone on stage.)*

BRUTUS. *(O.S.)* But it wasn't true?

WANDA. It was a catastrophe. I bought into my husband's lifestyle. I was willing to sacrifice everything that made me ME to make it a success with him. But the more I gave up of myself, the worse it got. In the end, I was just helping him hate me. If it wasn't for this old boyfriend who sort of rode in at the last minute, I would've been toast. I guess I have boundary issues. *(Brutus reappears suddenly.)*

BRUTUS. Who doesn't? After a certain point, select phrases should be banished from the public discourse. I nominate "boundary issues" for inclusion on the list.

WANDA. It describes a problem in contemporary relations.

BRUTUS. Just remember, in order to have boundaries, you've got to have territory!

WANDA. Good point.

BRUTUS. Identity.

WANDA. Yours seems fixed enough.

BRUTUS. I have several identities. There's the me when I'm alone. There's the me that exists in reaction to you.

WANDA. Me? What do I have to do with it?

BRUTUS. You are not me. You are other people.

WANDA. What other people?

BRUTUS. The other Face.

WANDA. You're getting obscure.

BRUTUS. When I encounter a person, have an encounter, it's like looking in the mirror and seeing, instead of myself, a stranger. That's my problem. I've never learned how to hear the voice of God while listening to the words of men. The difficulty of main-

taining my original soul. The danger of other people. For instance.
I can't pray while someone's looking at me not believing. I'm sus-
ceptible to doubt.

WANDA. So you pray.

BRUTUS. Don't you?

WANDA. Yes. I'm not devout the way my grandparents were, but
I say a prayer now and then.

BRUTUS. My father's faith is unshakable. He visited me here
once. He knelt in that spot and put his head ... *(Crooks his head
in a ritual manner.)* Made his devotion. Right here. And I knew
God could hear him. I memorized the moment. After he left, I
began to pray in that exact pose. In hopes God would mistake me
for my father. That's his hatbox. I keep it there. We all have our
little rituals. Have your coffee.

WANDA. You're very honest.

BRUTUS. I haven't got an honest bone in my body. I despise
honesty. Indirection, that's my modus.

WANDA. I think you underrate yourself.

BRUTUS. Do you? On what evidence?

WANDA. Well, you didn't like my work, you were rude, you blew
me off, but then you turn around, you relent, and you have the moral
courage to call me, extend an invitation to give it another shot.

BRUTUS. Let's face it. I was horrible the last time we talked.

WANDA. I have to tell you, I got in a cab and cried all the way
home.

BRUTUS. I'm sorry.

WANDA. I'm too sensitive.

BRUTUS. How can you be too sensitive? It's like a scalpel being
too sharp, a woman being too beautiful. *(Wanda, flustered, giggles.
Gets up.)*

WANDA. All my roommates say I'm too sensitive.

BRUTUS. How many roommates do you have?

WANDA. At the moment, just one. But I'm always moving. The
roommate thing is just ... I have that, you know, typically
American story. I have a family, but everybody lives somewhere
else and there's no ... village, you know? Someday I'm going to
have my own place. That's my dream. I decorate it in my head. I
was thinking about everything you said the other afternoon. You

really are brilliant at just RIFFING.

BRUTUS. Oh, but everything I say is response. Where's the action? Where's the vision? I can never wrestle myself free of context and give birth to something new. That's why I need isolation. I'm so easily contaminated by the pack. I need an idea that starts in the Present and goes into the Future. But all I do is defend and adjust and curse and worship what's already happened. I can't capitalize on Today. I can't grasp the Now. But it's worse even than that. Because I can't hold on to the Past, either. I've broken with everything. I'm in the soup.

WANDA. You have such an unusual tone. You're very definite, but everything you say seems to hint at something arcane.

BRUTUS. Maybe I know something that I can't say. It's like the story of the fish. Do you know the story of the fish?

WANDA. I don't think so.

BRUTUS. Once there was a young fish named Brutus in the middle of all the other young fish. And they went everywhere together. Well, of course they did. It was a school. So. One day, this bunch of little fish had congregated by a dock and they were arguing about … Well, it doesn't matter what they were arguing about. Because they shut up when they heard, up above, People! And they could hear little bits of what these people up above were saying. They kept mentioning "water." Our little school of fish was mystified. What was water? So Brutus said, "I don't know what water is, but I'm going to find out." And he set off. He left the school. Solo. Headed to the open sea. Years went by. Everyone forgot him. But then at last he returned. He was old now. Rusting hooks with bits of line trailed from his jaw. He moved slow, with a certain reluctant majesty. One of the oldest fish recognized him: "Is it you, Brutus? After all these years!" "Yes," he said. "It is me." "And did you find out, did you ever find out, what water is?" "Yes," he answered wearily. "Yes, I know what water is." "Well, since it's been the work of your whole life and we should all very much like to know, please tell us. What is water?" Brutus looked at them, one after the other, his old school, and shook his head. "You'd never believe me," he said. And then he swam away into the gloom.

WANDA. That's the end?

BRUTUS. Yes.

WANDA. It's sad.

BRUTUS. It is sad.

WANDA. Are you a sad man?

BRUTUS. I am more aggrieved than sad.

WANDA. The point of the story almost seems to be that knowledge alienates.

BRUTUS. Once you name a thing, nothing is ever the same.

WANDA. You named the fish after yourself. Your name's Brutus.

BRUTUS. Unless I'm named after the fish. The story's older than me. *(He goes to the cabinet, pours a shot of whiskey.)*

WANDA. How old are you?

BRUTUS. Old enough that my parents might outlive me. *(He downs the drink.)*

WANDA. Are you all right?

BRUTUS. Why would I be?!

WANDA. I'm so sorry. I didn't mean to offend.

BRUTUS. My fourth wife said "I'm sorry" all the time. You say you're sorry too much.

WANDA. I know. *(The steel shows through a moment.)* Someday I'm going to stop apologizing, then watch out. *(Pause.)* You've been married four times?

BRUTUS. Getting married repeatedly is like going to college. You learn a lot and the tuition just keeps going up. *(He heads off for the kitchen again.)*

WANDA. I watched the movie.

BRUTUS. *Frankenstein?*

WANDA. *The Perils of Pauline.* It's awful. Ridiculous.

BRUTUS. *(O.S.)* In what way?

WANDA. Well, it's unbelievable. Just one trumped-up situation after another. *(He reenters.)*

BRUTUS. You didn't identify with it?

WANDA. No!

BRUTUS. You can't understand the film unless you identify.

WANDA. Did you?

BRUTUS. Very much.

WANDA. Really?

BRUTUS. This is the pickle with your writing. You don't identify with your characters.

WANDA. But I absolutely deeply do!

BRUTUS. No.

WANDA. I worked on that book for sixteen months!

BRUTUS. They've been working on Sixth Avenue for twenty years. That doesn't make it a masterpiece.

WANDA. I am my characters.

BRUTUS. You bear no resemblance. Your characters are heroic cartoons.

WANDA. The movie was without merit.

BRUTUS. Obviously, you didn't understand the movie. Well, how could you? Pauline had curly blond hair. You don't know what that's like.

WANDA. You're not serious.

BRUTUS. I'm perfectly serious.

WANDA. Well, you don't have curly blond hair. Did you identify with her?

BRUTUS. Yes.

WANDA. How?

BRUTUS. I put on a wig.

WANDA. You did not!

BRUTUS. I put on a wig.

WANDA. You put on a curly blond wig and watched the movie?

BRUTUS. Yes.

WANDA. I don't believe you.

BRUTUS. You want to see?

WANDA. Yes, I do!

BRUTUS. All right. *(He reaches into the wardrobe, and pulls out a curly blond wig on a styrofoam head.)* See? Here it is.

WANDA. You do have a wig!

BRUTUS. I told you.

WANDA. You had that on your head?

BRUTUS. Yes. *(He puts the wig on.)* See?

WANDA. You watched the movie like that?

BRUTUS. So I could identify, yes.

WANDA. That's nuts.

BRUTUS. I do what I have to do. If I have to wear a wig, I wear a wig.

WANDA. And it really changed how you reacted to the character of Pauline?

BRUTUS. Of course. Completely. It makes you feel different to have curly blond ringlets.

WANDA. I wouldn't know. *(He takes it off and offers it to her.)*

BRUTUS. Put it on, look in the mirror, you'll feel differently. Go on.

WANDA. All right. *(She puts on the wig, looks in the mirror of the wardrobe.)*

BRUTUS. You're seeing somebody else now, right? It's not exactly you. You could pass for another person. Maybe even to yourself. You could pass. If you invest deeply enough.

WANDA. Do you seriously think my reaction to *The Perils of Pauline* would be different if I watched it in this wig?

BRUTUS. The wig's only a step, a gesture. It's just a hairpiece. We're trying to fool YOU. You're not so easily going to mistake yourself for Pauline. She did not identify with others. Her power came from the mirror.

WANDA. How do you mean?

BRUTUS. Pauline saw a world that contained only people like her. Reflections that wanted what she wanted, believed what she believed. Her peril and her strength was the same: She was ignorant of everything but Pauline. But you'd have to be more of a waif, wear a little waif dress.

WANDA. I suppose you wore something like that.

BRUTUS. That's right. I did. And here it is. Voilà. *(He pulls a white waif dress out.)*

WANDA. You wore a dress? You wore that dress?

BRUTUS. I did.

WANDA. It's very hard to take you seriously knowing that.

BRUTUS. It takes courage to be the right kind of fool. Put it on.

WANDA. What?

BRUTUS. Put the dress on.

WANDA. I will not!

BRUTUS. Come on. You're already wearing the wig. Think of what I was willing to do! I'm a man. You're a woman. It's much less for you to do it.

WANDA. For what I know you got off on wearing it!

BRUTUS. Just what I thought. You're totally unwilling to try on other points of view. That's why you stink as a writer. What are

26

you afraid of?

WANDA. I'd have to take my pants off.

BRUTUS. Oh, come on! You're ridiculous! Just throw it on over your precious jeans.

WANDA. But why?

BRUTUS. The fact that you find it so threatening should be reason enough! You're obviously afraid, entrenched, unimaginative, and bourgeois. You wanna know why your writing doesn't penetrate? Because it's just gutless. Words cost nothing. You need to risk something. You need to put your money down. I risked something to comprehend a woman's pain because I want to know! That's intellectual passion. That's what separates an artist from a woman sponge-painting her bathroom! *(She snatches the dress from him.)*

WANDA. Oh, all right, stop browbeating me! If your book hadn't convinced me that you were on to something exciting, there's no way in Hell I would be doing this!

BRUTUS. Admit it. You're doing it because you want to. You're making a choice. *(She assesses putting the dress on over the jeans and rejects the idea.)*

WANDA. This isn't going to work. Give me a minute. Stay out of the kitchen.

BRUTUS. Take your time. *(She exits. He takes a drink of wine, sings a bit of a folk song, finishes the glass. She laughs, Off.)* What?

WANDA. *(O.S.)* Never mind. Where'd you get this thing?

BRUTUS. Thrift shop.

WANDA. *(O.S.)* It scratches.

BRUTUS. It's Egyptian cotton.

WANDA. *(O.S.)* Those cotton-picking Egyptians. *(He sings a bit more. Drinks her wine.)*

BRUTUS. You need help?

WANDA. *(O.S.)* No!

BRUTUS. Too bad.

WANDA. *(O.S.)* Very funny. *(She reenters in the dress and wig.)* How do I look?

BRUTUS. Like a little moth.

WANDA. Where's that mirror?

BRUTUS. Very good. The mirror's the key to the whole thing. *(He presents her to herself in the mirror.)* Shazam. *(He starts away.)*

27

So you're looking … *(He goes to the cabinet. She likes something about the way she looks.)*

WANDA. Damn it. Jesus. I DO look like somebody else. *(He pulls out a little hat from the cabinet.)*

BRUTUS. There's a hat.

WANDA. A hat. All right. Give me the hat. I might as well shoot the moon. *(She puts on the hat.)*

BRUTUS. Now look in the mirror. Do you want to see her face? Do you want to see Pauline?

WANDA. Sure.

BRUTUS. You're going to have to be a lot more willing if you want to see something in yourself that you've never admitted before. Now do you want to see Pauline?

WANDA. Yes. Yes, I do.

BRUTUS. Do you contain goodness?

WANDA. Yes.

BRUTUS. And you contain evil. Look in there and forget me. Forget everything else. Look in that mirror and see there the whole world. Everything's there. Everything that's good, everything that's bad. That's true, isn't it?

WANDA. I guess it is.

BRUTUS. It's true. Now concentrate. This is a moral exercise. Look at what in you has value. Everything that has value. Everything worth defending, everything good. Look at that part of yourself, see that part of yourself, let everything else fall away, and say: "I am good."

WANDA. I am good.

BRUTUS. Keep looking in the mirror. "I am good."

WANDA. I am good.

BRUTUS. And you are. Look at that face. You can trust yourself, can't you? You know the best of yourself. Show that, like a shining shield, love that, ignore the rest and trust that.

WANDA. Okay. Okay.

BRUTUS. Very good. That's Pauline. You're Pauline. Your father left you a ranch. It's your birthright and it's all you have in the world. If I were to ask you, Pauline, under the threat of violence, for the deed to that ranch, what would you say? Give me the deed to your ranch.

28

WANDA. No.

BRUTUS. Hand over the deed to your father's ranch!

WANDA. I won't do it!

BRUTUS. I'm giving you one last chance to give over that deed!

WANDA. Never! Do you hear me! Though it should cost my life, you slobbering pig! You'll never get my poor dead dear father's ranch! This land is mine! *(Drops it.)* Wow!

BRUTUS. How was that?

WANDA. I feel kind of free.

BRUTUS. You've just realized you don't have to be you.

WANDA. But it was me!

BRUTUS. But it was you. Very good.

WANDA. I've never felt so in the right!

BRUTUS. That's it.

WANDA. Oh my God, I'd love to have a picture of this.

BRUTUS. You want a picture, I can take a picture.

WANDA. Really?

BRUTUS. No problem. I'm an excellent photographer. Actually, I do videos now, too. Would you like a video or a picture?

WANDA. A picture I think.

BRUTUS. I took the pictures in *Understanding Japanese*.

WANDA. You did? *(He gets a camera from the cabinet.)*

BRUTUS. Every one.

WANDA. They were very well composed.

BRUTUS. Sit in the chair. No, better! The ladder! *(He pulls the ladder Center.)* See? It's like the railroad tracks. *(She sits on it, poses.)*

WANDA. Like this?

BRUTUS. Try up one rung.

WANDA. Good?

BRUTUS. Good. So far. Now do you want the full experience?

WANDA. What would that be?

BRUTUS. In other words, a pose. Like Pauline would pose.

WANDA. How would she pose?

BRUTUS. Tied up. *(He pulls out a heavy rope. She hops off the ladder.)*

WANDA. No way.

BRUTUS. What is your problem? I'M not going to tie you up! Just you. Fake it. Lay the rope around your wrists. The camera can't tell the difference. *(He tosses her a bunch of rope.)*

WANDA. Oh. Okay. *(Returns to her perch, holds the rope against her.)* Sure. Something like that? How's that look?

BRUTUS. Fine. Now I need to see more violated trust. "Renounce your birthright!"

WANDA. No!

BRUTUS. "Denounce your patrimony!"

WANDA. No!

BRUTUS. Good! Now I'm going to put a glamorous light on you.

WANDA. Make me look good!

BRUTUS. Absolutely! *(He pulls the old studio light into place while singing a snatch of some romantic ditty. He turns it on. Then looks through the camera.)* But now the rope's wrong.

WANDA. What's wrong with it?

BRUTUS. It's slack. It's obvious that it's not ... *(He's been looking through the viewfinder. He abandons his post at the camera impatiently and comes over to her. He works on the rope for a second.)*

WANDA. Did I move it? Is that better?

BRUTUS. Not like that! Jesus! Here. Just make it believable. A couple of hitches or something. It can't be loose. It's got to be tight, tight, tight. Be brave. That should do it. Let's look at that. *(He goes back to look through the camera. She tries the rope, can't get free.)*

WANDA. Where's the knot? I can't reach the knot.

BRUTUS. No? I'll undo it in a minute. This looks much better.

WANDA. Undo it now. *(He heads to be cabinet hurriedly, grabs something.)* Absolutely! Just lemme just fix the background so the backlight is softer and ... PRESS. OPEN! *(He's pressed her jaw forcefully. It's painful.)* Ow! *(Her mouth pops open. He puts a ball gag in her mouth, pulls the band over her head. She tries to scream. It's quite a muffled sound.)*

BRUTUS. And that's as loud as you get, my dear. Not that anybody would hear you on this godforsaken avenue. Not that the hoi polloi would care if they did hear. *(He's tying her legs in such a way that they are spread wide.)* There's the East Side, there's the West Side, and then there's the Meat District, where everything's a candidate for dinner. You send me your selfish book. Your fantasy of an ideal world with you in the middle serving tea. I read every page. Do you know what I was looking for? Me. And guess what? I wasn't there. Shame on you. Fortunately, you're not the only one who dreams. And my fancies are more expansive than yours. Because in my perfect world, you show up. True, you're in a pickle. You're helpless. You're humiliated. You have no voice. But whose fault is that? Is there a greater provocation than to be ignored? I don't think so, but no matter. I've got you now. In MY dream. You don't want me in your club? Fine. You shut me out, I'll shut you down. *(Sings.)* What a day for a daydream. *(Drops it.)* But daydreams are fiction and fiction is dead, right? So let's set it up. Let's make it real. Why did you send me that book? Didn't you learn anything from your first go-round? Why are you here? Why did you step towards death again? Did you think I was going to jump for joy at your wonderful idea of a world without ME? Or was this what you were trolling for? Maybe you recognize all of this. The ropes, the feeling, the fear. Did you enlist me to do this for you, you pixie? Did you seek me out to do this for you? When we met, I was playing chess alone. It's hard to play both parts, isn't it? It can be done, but it's hard to be both the Villain and the Victim, and experience the FULL understanding. *(He's been adjusting his clothing, changing into the Villain. He puts on protective goggles. Now he reaches into the wardrobe and pulls out a circular saw.)* So you don't get it? You can't identify with Pauline? A woman tied to the railroad tracks, a train coming towards her. The ringlets. The frock! It's absurd, right? Contrived. *(He starts up the circular saw. It roars to life. She's trying to scream, tears running down her face. He cuts a two-by-four in half.)* WELL, HONEY, YOU WILL IDENTIFY WITH PAULINE! YOU HEAR ME!!! IF YOU EVER GET TO WATCH THAT MOVIE AGAIN, TRUST ME, TRUST ME, YOU WILL BE ON THE EDGE OF YOUR SEAT!!! *(He turns toward her with the saw, heads for her belly. She screams, screams. Blackout. The headlight of the train [the old studio light] bears down on us. The roaring sound of a train builds, the whistle screaming. Then sudden silence.)*

Scene 3

The "Moonlight Sonata" begins to play. The old studio light burns dimly. Brutus enters the darkened room with a candelabra of lit candles. Wanda has fainted. A second shorter ladder has been set up by the first.

BRUTUS. Hello? Hi. You fainted. The "Moonlight Sonata." So now you know something. Now you've had an experience. Something concrete. You're in the soup. You've been living in your head too long. Don't you feel better? *(She looks at her stomach, realizes he didn't cut her. She whimpers with relief.)* No, I didn't cut you up. Actually, WE'VE had an experience. That's right. Now there's a WE. We have a relationship. There's a bond. Maybe I'll give you a nickname. Any suggestions? Good idea. Nipples. Let's just put some clips on those. One. And two. *(He's put clips on her nipples.)* Two of the three points of the triangle. I wonder how the third point is doing? The Delta. *(Climbs the second ladder.)* But back to Pauline. She's tied to the tracks. SHE'S not gagged. What do you think she really says to the Villain once she sees the train in the distance? The danger jacking up each moment. At first, certainly, she appeals to his humanity, his decency. But when that falls flat, she undoubtedly speaks to him as a Man. She offers herself to him. Of course she doesn't mean it! She's just trying to save herself. But as the approaching train's vibration starts to rage like a hyena through her body, and the concept that this guy is her only hope solidifies into certainty, doesn't it seem likely that her pretense of lust would terrify down into lust itself? That the fiction of her civilized character would start to fall apart? That she would begin, in the savage grip of self-interest, to genuinely experience a ravenous desperate desire to please this man, to indulge this man, if only he will save her? She makes promises. Terrible, beautiful promises ... And while she's says these things, her voice, competing with the train, rises in intensity, in sincerity, in depth of conviction. Until finally, she breaks through. And she offers to die for him. She loves him. She loves him so much. She is so utterly committed to his will. She is content to die for him beneath the wheels of the oncoming train. All she asks is a single kiss. And at that moment of perfect subjugation, the Villain unties her and drags her limp body off the tracks, and fucks her. He fucks her even as the train roars by like madness. He takes her with such vulturine bloodlust that for a moment the past does not exist. There's only the Now. And her white dress in ruins. He upchucks obscenities, gushes fluids, voids rages, floods her womb, marks her psyche, soils, begrimes everything that could be said to BE her. Until she's done to the brim. Full. And he's empty. And then he's finished. His clutch loosens, his eyes glaze, his body becomes indifferent. He stands, pulls up his pants, wipes himself off on the tail of his shirt, and starts walking home. As if you'd never existed. You look after him. You make your way to your feet. And. You. Follow him. *(Pause. With a remote, he shuts off the "Sonata.")* And here we are. You and me. In reality. I tell you this tale. You can't speak. Your legs are spread. You listen to this story of the girl on the train tracks. And so many things pass through your mind to say to me, some scornful, some pleading, some accommodating. But you are enjoined through circumstance to remain silent. Your inner journey's mysterious conclusion unknown even to you. Because a process endured without benefit of civilized response leads to an outcome beyond the imagination of thought. *(He takes the gag out of her mouth. Dabs her lips with a handkerchief.)* Let me take this out. What do you want me to do, Wanda? How do you want me to treat you now? *(A sledgehammer hits the door from outside once, twice. At the third blow, the door falls down. Dust rises. A slim handsome cowboy, Frank, is standing there with a sledgehammer, which he casts aside. He surfs down the fallen door and pulls his gun.)*

FRANK. Hold it right there, Mister!

BRUTUS. Who are you? Don't shoot! I'm unarmed! I'm an unarmed man! *(Frank throws a massive breaker switch by the door. A photoflash comes out of the breaker and the all the lights in the loft bang up.)*

FRANK. Stand away from that goddamn girl! *(Brutus blinks at the brightness. Frank strides over to Wanda, unties her, asking.)* Are you

33

okay, Wanda?

WANDA. Frank? *(She's in shock. She pulls off the nipple clips and throws them down.)*

BRUTUS. You know her?

FRANK. That's right. She's a friend of mine.

WANDA. How did you find me, Frank?

FRANK. Your Aunt Zelda had a bad feeling. Gave me the address.

BRUTUS. I think you should go before I call the police. As you can see, Wanda is fine.

FRANK. She is not fine, asshole! She's in shock. What the hell's the matter with you?! What the hell did you do to her? *(Wanda puts her hands on the Frank's chest.)* You okay? *(She pushes him away.)*

WANDA. Fuck off, Frank. Mind your own business. I'm a big girl now and I'll handle this my own way. You understand English, Frank?! GET OUT and leave us to it!

FRANK. But he's ... he ...

WANDA. It's not like before. I'll deal with this ... one. In my own way. I can handle it. Get out. *(Frank takes a step towards the doorway, hesitates.)*

FRANK. Are you sure?

BRUTUS. Don't feel bad, Frank. It's modern life. Either you're the Villain or the Victim. Those are the only roles available. No one is exempt.

WANDA. One favor. Leave me the gun.

FRANK. All right. Good enough. *(Frank hands her the gun.)* Hasta Luego. *(Frank exits.)*

BRUTUS. Now where were we?

WANDA. First of all, I don't want you to call me Nipples.

BRUTUS. All right. What do you want me to call you? *(She lifts the gun. She takes on a new wildness, a new nobility.)*

WANDA. Call. Me. Israel. *(Blackout.)*

ACT TWO

Scene 1

Music. The cowboy, Frank, sits at a bar tossing cards into his hat. He's gained a lot of weight. Watson, the bartender, a Cockney, looks on. It's the same guy who played Lawrence; he raises a sign that says: NONFICTION. The music fades, replaced by Frank singing. Watson sweeps up.

FRANK. CAMP TOWN RACES SING THIS SONG
WATSON. DO DAH! DO DAH!
FRANK. CAMP TOWN RACE IS WAY TOO LONG
WATSON. OH DA DO DAH DAY!
FRANK. GOIN' TO RUN ALL NIGHT
WATSON. Right.
FRANK. GOIN' TO RUN ALL DAY
WATSON. True.
FRANK. BET MY MONEY ON A BOB-TAILED NAG
WATSON. Ouch.
FRANK. SOMEBODY BET ON THE GRAY
WATSON. Tragic, isn't it?
FRANK. No customers. Not a single goddamn customer. What happened to the drinking public?
WATSON. Take it easy. Why would there be any customers, Frank? It's Sunday morning and we're closed.
FRANK. Maybe we should open?
WATSON. The law says no serving of alcoholic beverages on Sunday morning. It's to promote churchgoing I believe.
FRANK. Church. You go?
WATSON. Not for years. You?
FRANK. Sometimes, but I have trouble with it.

35

WATSON. Doubt?

FRANK. No, envy. I don't wanna worship, I wanna preach.

WATSON. It's my impression that religions were organized AGAINST God. Like labor unions.

FRANK. Labor unions! Are you trying to get my goat?!

WATSON. Not a bit.

FRANK. Are you trying to get health benefits?!

WATSON. No, no! I have a perfectly nice little first aid kit! *(Watson has fled behind the bar. Frank starts as if he heard something. Impasse.)*

FRANK. Can't you feel it?

WATSON. What?

FRANK. The silence.

WATSON. Maybe you should *(Knocks.)* let it in?

FRANK. I don't think so, kimosabe. I prefer noise and toys. *(Frank pulls out a pack of cigarettes and slams them on the bar.)* Try this on.

WATSON. What's this?

FRANK. Pack a cigarettes.

WATSON. What good's that do me? I don't smoke.

FRANK. Maybe you could start.

WATSON. Why?

FRANK. Try one on the house.

WATSON. Why would I do that?

FRANK. You might like it.

WATSON. Bloody Hell, so much the worse. I get addicted. Do you smoke?

FRANK. I quit. That shit'll kill ya.

WATSON. I don't want the cigarettes. *(Frank snatches the pack back.)*

FRANK. All right, so don't have one.

WATSON. Well, you don't have to be like that about it.

FRANK. Oh, I don't, huh?

WATSON. It's just that they make me cough.

FRANK. You begrudge me makin' a livin'?

WATSON. You do all right.

FRANK. So everybody thinks.

WATSON. What's the matter?

FRANK. What do you care?

WATSON. You don't seem to be your jolly self.

FRANK. You ever feel like the old tricks aren't working?

WATSON. I was born feeling that way.

FRANK. Like a monkey on a chain dancing for apathetic children.

WATSON. Poor little monkey.

FRANK. I'm suffering, Watson.

WATSON. From what?

FRANK. Well. In a few words. I'm a very social person and I feel isolated.

WATSON. Okay. I see. So you're down.

FRANK. Exactly! I'm down, Watson. I'm as down as I've ever been, and I hate it. I prefer to be happy. Well, what the hell is that? Who doesn't want to be happy?

WATSON. Lots of people.

FRANK. Really? Why?

WATSON. Otherwise engaged.

FRANK. And then there's my weight.

WATSON. You look fine.

FRANK. I'm fat. Wherever I go, I'm the fattest person in the room.

WATSON. A few pounds is all.

FRANK. I used to be as slinky as a puma. It's all part of the depression.

WATSON. Is that why you took to drugs?

FRANK. Why do you go right to that? I've cleaned up. Been through the Program three and a half times. *(Frank pops a pill.)*

WATSON. What's that you just took?

FRANK. Psychopharmaceutical.

WATSON. What's it do?

FRANK. Do I look like a M.D.? Goddammit, you've gotta have some faith, Watson! How 'bout a slice a lemon? *(Watson goes off for lemon.)* This atmosphere of cynicism is killing me! It's not just you. It's the attitude on every park bench. Look at me. I got something better to offer, but the problem is: it seems like nobody wants it. *(Watson reenters with lemon.)*

WATSON. You mean cigarettes?

FRANK. No! I'm talkin' about something intangible and fine. I'm talkin' about my heart. I'm talkin' about my soul. You know what I'm talking about? I'm talkin' about my philosophy.

WATSON. I didn't even know you had a philosophy.

FRANK. How do you think I became a success? It's because I

operate from a philosophy.

WATSON. Well, what is it?

FRANK. Me. My philosophy is me. I believe I'm the best so that's what I sell. My message is simple: Be like me. Do like I do. And it works. I'm an idea, I put that idea out there, and people like the idea. The only problem is: People don't like me. They like the idea of me, they try to do like I do, but when they come face to face with the original article, their smile goes crocodile. The upshot? Well, take a gander. I'm alone. Success, yes. But what friends I have are bought and paid for. Nobody just likes me.

WATSON. What about your cronies?

FRANK. A man wearies of cronies.

WATSON. Well, I like you. Lots of people like you.

FRANK. I don't feel it.

WATSON. You want love.

FRANK. That's it. I want love, and nobody loves me.

WATSON. Can't help you there.

FRANK. Why not?

WATSON. It's not that I don't admire you, Frank. I do. I'd like to be you. I'd like to be sitting where you are, and you going about serving me.

FRANK. Well, that's how it was when I was a kid, remember? I used to sweep up and you'd be reading the paper.

WATSON. Those were the days. I thought they'd never end. Why did they end?

FRANK. I remember why. It's the day I made that cup a tea, and you charged me twice.

WATSON. I didn't charge you twice. Up until that point, I'd been giving us both the company discount. That day I decided to retain the discount for management, and abolish the discount for labor. You took it all wrong.

FRANK. It was unfair.

WATSON. Haven't you ever done anything unfair?

FRANK. Not that I like to remember.

WATSON. You overreacted.

FRANK. I by God stood up and took my place at table. I love you, Watson, but you're a son of a bitch when you've got the whip.

WATSON. Who isn't?

FRANK. Me.

WATSON. Hubris. First step on the slippery slope.

FRANK. You're right and I hear ya. That's why it's so good having you around.

WATSON. The voice of experience.

FRANK. Why, I can look at your face and see every mistake I might ever make.

WATSON. That's me. I'm a cautionary tale.

FRANK. You're a tonic is what you are! Just lookin' at the second-rate state you're in gives me a boost!

WATSON. We have a bond.

FRANK. That's right! Goddammit, we do have a bond! We have a special relationship. *(Pulls out a pistol, hands it to Watson.)* Here. What do you think a that shootin' stick? It's a beauty, ain't it?

WATSON. I can't afford to buy any more guns from you, Frank. I still owe you for the car.

FRANK. You love that car though, don't ya?

WATSON. It is a treat.

FRANK. Just feel the action.

WATSON. Why, when you're anxious, do you always resort to the sales pitch?

FRANK. Careful now. My daddy always said: "Guns are like Irishmen. Assume they're loaded." *(Watson has a good laugh.)*

WATSON. Ah, I do love a joke at the expense of the Irish. It is a nice little gun. Take it back. *(Watson puts the gun down.)*

FRANK. You don't have to pay me anytime soon. Shit, you don't have to pay me at all. Not in money anyways.

WATSON. Then how?

FRANK. I don't know. Wash my back sometime.

WATSON. I can't make up my mind about you.

FRANK. How so?

WATSON. Faust or the Devil? *(Frank puts the gun in Watson's hand during the next line.)*

FRANK. Either way, we're in business. *(Indicating gun.)* Man, you look good with that iron Marlboro in your hand. You look like me. Wyatt Earp always said: "When you reach for a weapon and it ain't there, it's too late."

WATSON. Did Wyatt Earp really say that?

FRANK. Who cares? He's dead. Why don't you put that little piece a punctuation where you can reach it, if and when, so's you don't get caught short.

WATSON. All right. Better safe than sorry I suppose. *(Watson stows the pistol under the bar.)*

FRANK. That's the way. Deal done. Nothin's quite got the snap of a good transaction. What do you think? You want me to stand you to a drink? C'mon, I'll buy you a drink. *(Frank is about to pour a shot. Watson blocks the glass with his palm.)*

WATSON. I can't have a drink. I'd lose me job.

FRANK. Right. I did make that rule, and it is a good rule. But if I don't buy you a drink, maybe you'll start to hate me.

WATSON. You're so insecure.

FRANK. Wouldn't you be? No roots. Born in an orphanage. Everybody's child, nobody's son. That's my birth scar.

WATSON. What do you give a damn what other people think of you?

FRANK. What do they think of me?

WATSON. Who?

FRANK. Well, like your buddies.

WATSON. Oh, they think you're all right.

FRANK. No, they don't! Just all right, huh?

WATSON. Well, the Frenchman, he's never going to get on with you.

FRANK. Louie? Why not?

WATSON. He thinks you're gauche.

FRANK. Gauche.

WATSON. Go on. Ask me what it means.

FRANK. I don't care what it means.

WATSON. It means you're an awkward, embarrassing, clumsy person.

FRANK. Oh I am, huh? You know that a amphibian wants to eat like me, dress like me, and drive an SUV! And when the hell's he gonna give up speakin' French anyway?

WATSON. It's his language.

FRANK. It's pretentious. You don't speak in French.

WATSON. That's true.

FRANK. But you oughta lose that accent. You can if you put your mind to it. Practice speakin' like me.

WATSON. Take my advice. Don't bother about Louie. He's just jealous. There's nothing you can do about that.

FRANK. But I want him to like me!

WATSON. Why?

FRANK. I don't know. I wanna shine. That's the way I am. I wanna shine. So maybe I try too hard. Try to win everybody over. Try and try. But then I gotta tell you, this other thing kicks in, and I get full-up disgusted. Hate everybody. I think: Fuck 'em all. Who needs 'em? I go to my apartment, shut the door. Keep to myself. And cook. That's my passion.

WATSON. I didn't know that. You're a cook?

FRANK. I have to cook 'cause I love to eat. You know what the key to cooking is? Ingredients.

WATSON. Do you know what the problem with eating is: The more you eat, the more you want to eat.

FRANK. I give up cigarettes. I'm off the drugs. I gotta have something.

WATSON. When are you going to sit down with yourself and address your restless soul?

FRANK. Never. Sometimes I have a moment when this silence wraps itself around me like an anaconda. And I feel the Hate out there. I look up to the sky for comfort and see the majority is darkness and cold, and that the stars are ignorant and do not care. And that, that's when I have a major chowdown. And as I eat my way to that latest plateau of satiety, the loneliness fades to gold. It's a new day. And I begin to fantasize about what the world COULD be. Don't you sometimes wish we could all sit down and bare our souls and get to some kind of deeper understanding?

WATSON. No.

FRANK. You don't?

WATSON. No.

FRANK. But how could you not want that, Watson?

WATSON. Well, to begin with, it would ruin the poker game.

FRANK. I don't even like poker.

WATSON. You can't kid me. You invented poker. There's that woman again.

FRANK. Who?

WATSON. There's this woman been looking in the window the last few days, but she never comes in.

FRANK. Jesus.

WATSON. What?

FRANK. I know her. Have you ever had a woman where you didn't know where to put her in your head? Where there's a chemistry so intense you can't afford to fuck her and you'd die if you cut her loose?

WATSON. I kind of feel that way about the Queen.

FRANK. She is like a Queen this one, a Queen in trouble, like some Cleopatra. But she's also something altogether new. A new kind of monarch brought to flower in the blood-soaked garden of world guilt. She's a dream, a folktale, her existence justified by prophecies and firepower. A thousand rivers from a hundred countries feed the headwaters of her soul. She's inevitable, impossible, the embodiment of Justice done. I'm telling you, the gods themselves fall back in fear that the hand of man has occasionally forged such a one as this. For when you make an ideal real, the blood will spill like adolescent tears. Is there anything more dangerous than a dream literally realized? Is there anything more … Romantic? *(Music. The theme from* Exodus *or* Chariots of Fire *or some such sweeping orchestral arrangement.* Wanda makes a big entrance. She's no longer dressed like a graduate student. Now she's in a graceful gown and sunglasses. Frank gets up, takes off his hat, dances with Wanda. The music stops and they stop with it.)*

WANDA. Hi. *(He shoves her away, acting like a spurned lover.)*

FRANK. What do you want?

WANDA. I just thought we might catch up. Can I get a beer?

WATSON. We're closed.

FRANK. Watson, serve her up.

WATSON. All right then. *(Serves her.)* Happy New Year. I'll be in the basement putting down poison for the squeakies. *(Watson exits.)*

WANDA. How long's it been?

FRANK. Since when?

WANDA. How long have we known each other?

FRANK. Your whole life.

WANDA. Not that long.

FRANK. Round it off. Your whole life and we have yet to settle a

* See Special Note on Songs and Recordings on copyright page.

goddamn thing.

WANDA. Time flies. How you doing?

FRANK. Terrific. Business is booming. Ain't sellin' the smokes like I did, but everybody loves the guns.

WANDA. You always had the knack. Good for you. You put on a couple of pounds.

FRANK. I know. I'm fat.

WANDA. I didn't say that.

FRANK. *(Tapping his shirt pocket.)* It's a side effect.

WANDA. Of what? *(She pulls a vial of pills out his pocket, chucks it.)* What do you need that shit for?

FRANK. When you've been singing up-tempo as long as me, sometimes you need a little help.

WANDA. You're better than that.

FRANK. I guess better ain't good enough. Congratulations on the book.

WANDA. Thanks.

FRANK. Never gave up.

WANDA. Paid off.

FRANK. Bestseller?

WANDA. No. Lotta people hate it. But a loyal following.

FRANK. How's the household side a life?

WANDA. Nothing much.

FRANK. Fibber McGee.

WANDA. All right. I just don't know how to start.

FRANK. Why not start at the leave off? I untied you, gave you a gun. You had the drop on that creep. When I left, you were hooked up like Marge in charge. How'd it play out?

WANDA. I was rude to you.

FRANK. Doesn't bother me. I wrote you off.

WANDA. No, you didn't.

FRANK. I should have.

WANDA. I was asserting myself. I wanted to stand on my own. You want me to stand on my own, don't you?

FRANK. I don't know. I admire independence, but I like bein' needed. So what happened?

WANDA. I got to the point, I thought I could work it out with him.

FRANK. Well, good for you. I like that. Optimism.

WANDA. I couldn't.

FRANK. Don't beat yourself up. Let me tell you something. At the end of the day, Yes will triumph over No. So how's it shakin' down?

WANDA. A no-holds-barred, twenty-four-car domestic train wreck.

FRANK. Damn. Well then, maybe you should leave.

WANDA. Where would I go?

FRANK. Good point. It's tight out there.

WANDA. He should leave.

FRANK. Isn't it his place?

WANDA. It was, but now it's ours. And actually, I have a prior claim. *(Pulls a piece of paper out of her garter.)* My grandfather lived there long before this guy.

FRANK. He did?

WANDA. And the wording of my grandfather's lease suggests I have rights. I love the apartment. It's the first real home I've had in a very long time. But I'm not going to lie to you. I'm in trouble. I'm going to lose it unless I get some kind of help.

FRANK. You mean money?

WANDA. I mean more than money.

FRANK. So you mean money.

WANDA. I'm talking about something more.

FRANK. Somebody's cashing the checks I send.

WANDA. And I thank you. But I need something more.

FRANK. You're losing me. More than money? What are we talking about?

WANDA. I need Justice. *(Watson enters with a case of Coke.)*

WATSON. And you came to Frank?

FRANK. What's that supposed to mean?

WATSON. Just popped out. *(Watson ducks out of sight behind the bar.)*

WANDA. Look. I'm a proud person. I put myself through college. I work two jobs. I try to make my own way. But I'm having to defend myself against somebody who's just got nothing else to do. This guy's been unemployed for like a century. His life's a disaster and he's decided to blame me.

FRANK. What's he at? *(The unseen Watson puts four six-packs of Coke on the bar, one after the other.)*

WANDA. It's not just him. He has this intense family. And they all have trust funds and grudges the size of Norway. They have blood feuds with the dry cleaner these guys.

FRANK. I know his family. *(Watson pops up.)*

WATSON. The Chiappas. They're tougher than Turkish taffy.

FRANK. They are a little testy. *(Watson disappears again.)*

WANDA. Well, the thing is, they all hate me. They got this dead-beat relative and they blame me. They think I'm the problem. And they're willing to pay any amount of money to harass me and get me to move out. I have nobody I can go to. Except you. Everybody hates me except you.

FRANK. Why's everybody hate you?

WANDA. I have no idea. It's just been an historic fact. I must stand for something that I don't even know about. Look, it's a natural thing to want to be independent. Since the day I was born I've depended on you. I'd like that to end. But I need you.

FRANK. And you hate me for it!

WANDA. I don't hate you.

FRANK. No?

WANDA. No.

FRANK. Goddammit, why do I care!

WANDA. You have to care, Frank. It's the only thing that saves you from being a monster.

FRANK. I'm fightin' to keep my hands off you.

WANDA. I feel things, too.

FRANK. But it's always mixed up with money.

WANDA. Are you calling me a whore?

FRANK. If I was poor, would you even talk to me?

WANDA. What do you think?

FRANK. I don't know. I don't want to get involved again. Everything's messy with you. I like to keep things simple. *(Watson pops up from behind the bar, grabbing a pack of soda.)*

WATSON. Some people think you're stupid. *(Watson disappears.)*

FRANK. Well, if I'm stupid, how come I'm doing better than everybody else? *(Watson reappears to grab more soda. Stays up this time.)*

WATSON. Some people say it's because you're very lucky.

FRANK. I believe you make your own luck.

WATSON. The people on top always do.

FRANK. And the people on the bottom always talk shit. I wonder

45

how well you'd treat me, Watson, if you were in my shoes. I remember the way it was. I remember what kind of boss you were. I would never treat a man the way you treated me. *(To her.)* He charged me twice for a cuppa tea!

WATSON. Blimey, I'm sorry about the bloody tea! You're like an elephant! I apologize, I was strapped. I needed cash.

FRANK. It was unjust.

WATSON. Haven't you ever done anything unjust?

FRANK. Not that I like to remember.

WATSON. If I had another shot at things, I'm sure I'd do better.

FRANK. I'm not.

WATSON. I've become understanding of the underdog.

FRANK. That's because you are the underdog!

WATSON. I'd like to think I've learned a bit since the sun set on my supermarket.

FRANK. The only thing that made you compassionate was come-uppance.

WATSON. No, I mean it, Frank! Look at me. I'm sincere. I've changed.

FRANK. Have you?

WATSON. Yes.

FRANK. I swear to God I want to believe you, Buddy. You're the closest thing to a father I never had.

WATSON. You know I think of you as a son.

FRANK. When we squabble, it eats me up. We're a family. Families should be able to work things out.

WATSON. It's about Trust now.

FRANK. That's right. You've gotta trust me.

WATSON. No, you've got to trust me.

FRANK. Me first.

WATSON. All right. I'm willing to make the gesture. Listen. If you decide you want to help this woman, I'm in. Anything you need.

FRANK. Are you serious?

WATSON. Deadly serious. All my resources. At your disposal.

FRANK. Now are you saying that because I'm a good customer, and your boss, and you owe me money for the gun, or are you saying that because we're friends.

WATSON. Because we're friends, of course.

46

FRANK. Well, I'm moved, Watson. I'm deeply moved. *(They embrace.)*

WANDA. So you'll help me? *(Frank shoves Watson away, finished with him. Watson goes behind the bar during the next; unseen by Frank, he pours himself a shot and knocks it back.)*

FRANK. I didn't say that. I'm just seeing how things line up. You got that grandfather lease with you? *(She pulls out a paper and hands it to him.)*

WANDA. Yeah. Take a look. I've got a tidy little case there. *(He looks it over while talking.)*

FRANK. You're telling me the claim is legitimate?

WANDA. My people were there first.

FRANK. Good! I like that. That's strong. Plain. If you can't say it in ten seconds, what's the point? Tell me something, Princess. Smart as you are, pretty as you are, how come I'm the only person who likes you?

WANDA. How should I know? I've always tried to get along. But people have this weird reaction to me.

WATSON. I can understand that. You seem kind of, I don't know, up to something. Shifty. What's your game?

WANDA. You see? This is exactly what I'm talking about. This.

WATSON. You can't fool me, ladylove. You're in on something. There's some kind of plot or conspiracy, an international secret cabala protocol. I'm a bit of a scholar, you know. I read pamphlets.

WANDA. Don't I have a right to an apartment?

FRANK. Well, let's say you're correct. Let's say you do have a claim. Obviously, he has one, too. He lives there.

WANDA. I'm not telling him to move.

FRANK. You're not?

WANDA. No.

FRANK. Oh. Okay.

WANDA. But there is the question of stuff.

FRANK. What stuff?

WANDA. He has stuff and I have stuff, but I have more stuff and nicer stuff than he has so I think that I should have more of the apartment than he does.

FRANK. Well, that's just crazy.

WANDA. No, it's not.

FRANK. Yes, it is.

WATSON. I agree with Frank.

WANDA. Suckass.

FRANK. Did you make a smart remark?

WANDA. Of course not.

WATSON. Yes, you did. And it hurt. Ow.

FRANK. Please be careful with Watson's feelings. We have a special relationship.

WANDA. I apologize. *(Watson puts out his hands to Frank with a gooey look in his eyes.)*

WATSON. Hands? *(Frank takes Watson's hands.)*

FRANK. Hands across the water, buddy.

WATSON. You know I love you, man.

FRANK. Back at ya. *(Through with him.)* Gimme some peanuts.

WANDA. So you'll help me?

FRANK. Well, there is a sticking point.

WANDA. What?

FRANK. Oil. The Chiappa family makes my favorite olive oil.

WANDA. Well, what's more important? I mean, I don't want to exaggerate, but I could be killed. These people are ruthless. I live in fear.

FRANK. I know you have a problem, but this is some rum tum yummy olive oil. I've cooked with butter, I've cooked with Crisco. But I gotta tell you, once I tried Chiappa's olive oil, there was no goin' back.

WANDA. So Brutus was right. You're not a hero.

FRANK. You're a little quick to disenchant. Motivations non-withstanding, a man does an heroic thing, why isn't he a hero?

WANDA. Because he gets something out of it.

FRANK. And is that a problem?

WANDA. You want the man to untie the woman from the rail-road tracks because it's the right thing to do, not because he's going to benefit.

FRANK. If I untie a woman from the tracks, I'd like to think I'd get a little kiss, if not a good twenty-four-hour fuck session. Otherwise, why get up in the morning?

WANDA. So you won't help me?

FRANK. I didn't say that. I'm going to try to find a way to help you AND have my salad the way I like it. Can a check solve this? Can I write you both a smart little check?

WANDA. I told you. Just money isn't going to work.

FRANK. Why not?

WANDA. I hate his fucking guts and he wants me dead.

FRANK. How about I give you both a whole shitload a guns?

WANDA. No.

FRANK. Dammit. So what's gotta happen?

WANDA. Dominate us. Tell us what to do.

WATSON. So Frank would be kind of a sexual dungeon master or something? You are a naughty girl. Watch out, Frank. Deep waters.

FRANK. Watson's right. Why me? Why would I get involved in something so unwholesome? Why would I do that?

WANDA. Because you love me.

FRANK. No. (*He starts to walk away, resisting her. She lifts her hand, stopping him with the theme that played earlier; it underscores this next speech.*)

WANDA. Most people just take up where their parents left off, Frank. Most people just look at their shoes. But you and me, we're pioneers. We lift our eyes and look out ahead. We rejected the tyranny of the Past and fell in love with the freedom of the Future. Out of the rough stuff of injustice, we resolved to make practical an ideal. We were dealt with unfairly. Yes. But it made us dream of a better way of life, a place where we would no longer be persecuted. You fought to make a place like that for yourself. I'm fighting for that place now. We call that place Home. (*Frank turns to her, takes her in an embrace.*)

FRANK. Goddammit, you can play me like a jukebox! I'm with you, baby. (*Music ends.*) Lemme give you somethin', I wanna give you somethin'. Lemme give you a tank!

WANDA. No! You're a madman! (*Frank pulls out a big, toy remote-controlled tank and presents it to her.*)

FRANK. Here, factory fresh. This is primo. You're gonna love it! It's all-terrain!

WANDA. Wow. Thank you, Frank.

WATSON. I've got three. They're great!

FRANK. Try it! Hit the switch! (*She sends the tank whizzing around the bar floor.*)

WANDA. Oh, I love this thing!

FRANK. I knew you would. It's got a big motor.

WANDA. Like you.

FRANK. Hush up with that.

WANDA. Can I count on your help with the apartment? *(Music. The theme from* The Magnificent Seven *or some other big Western movie starts to play.* Frank considers, Wanda hopes, Frank takes her hands, then pulls her to him, committed, all to the music. Watson sets about closing up.)*

FRANK. Let's go straighten this doubledealing cocksucker out. Close up shop, Watson. I'm callin' in my chits. This is a sticky ball a rice and I may need chopsticks.

WATSON. Just as you say.

FRANK. Let's ride! *(Frank mounts an imaginary horse, Wanda gets on behind him, and Watson jumps on last. The horse whinnies three times as they rear to the left, to the right, and then straight back. The music continues. Frank does a Yeehaa! and they ride off, exiting. Wanda reenters, still in music, retrieves her tank, which she holds aloft in glory; then she puts it down, operates the remote, and drives it off. The music segues into the sound of a real tank as she exits and ...)*

Scene 2

... Brutus enters from opposite side of the stage to moody music with an Arabian flavor. He is carrying his father's hatbox. He puts it down, and takes out and dons an Arab headdress. Then he rolls the old movie light into place, turns it on. Lastly, he sets up a little video camera on its stand. He takes his place before the camera.

BRUTUS. Take number seventeen. The Goodbye Video. *(He gets in character.)* How long can a man live off good memories? How long before he needs something new? The time is now. I want to say … to my father … When you see this, I am already dead. You never appreciated my scholarship. I know that. You called me a girl for reading books. Well, I'm not reading books anymore. I am a man of action now. Perhaps you will raise your opinion of me. To my mother, You are no doubt shedding fat tears of sorrow and regret and counting the insurance money you've collected. For the many times you did not love me, for valuing my death more than my life, I want to say to you: I am in Paradise. I am surrounded by virgins and candy and raisins and God is here with me and He doesn't like you very much. But I am not angry anymore. I speak to you from a place beyond anger. I am free. To my wider family, I want to say look at me, how terrific it is to be me, and why don't you all just hope to be as brave and good as I am. And goodbye. And cut. *(Drops character.)* And fuck you for making me destroy myself. *(The lights crossfade to the sounds of English backbenchers booing. Brutus remains in shadow, his head lowered. Fade up on Watson on a microphone talking to his constituents, the audience.)*

WATSON. Please. Please! My countrymen! I know, I know! I know the question that's on all of your minds. I say it right out: Why do I always side with Frank? Nobody else sides with Frank except when it suits them. Frank sends them money, they take the money, they abuse him anyway. So why am I always shoulder to shoulder with the bloke? The answer is, I do it for you. If I stand next to Frank, if I court the strong and bully the weak, if I walk when he walks, judge when he judges, kill when he kills, if I talk morality and act in self-interest LONG ENOUGH, one day I will eat Frank and I will burp and then I will be Frank. And you, my brethren, will be able to reclaim your paramount position in the community. Is it difficult to blend completely with a man so unlike meself? Yes. But I have discovered that many of his movements come quite naturally to me. Many of his actions are not foreign to me at all.

FRANK'S VOICE. Hey you! Hey! Over here! *(Brutus directs the tripod light to pick out Frank in the aisle. Frank appears in a tux, bow tie undone, with a mike of his own.)*

FRANK. And I'd just like to say … *(Franks starts singing "You Light Up My Life" or "Take It to the Limit" or some such thing.* He joins Watson on stage. Watson joins Frank now, making it a duet. The*

---

* See Special Note on Songs and Recordings on copyright page.

sound of a record scratching interrupts them, followed by a hard-rock instrumental. They start dancing, blackout. Another record scratch takes us into ...)

Scene 3

Frantic French rock and roll. Something like "Ca Plane Pour Ma" by Plastic Bertrand. An image in the darkness: a spot up on the Devil dancing. The light goes out. Spot on Wanda, in the doorway, who dances like a military go-go goddess demanding tribute. She's wearing a red beret, camouflage pants, holstered gun and a tanktop. She gestures, conjuring Brutus' entrance; he's in his headdress. He throws open each of the three sets of shutters in turn. Each time he does this, there is a flash of light and an explosion, from which he staggers back. He reaches Wanda and mock spanks her in a rage, while she acts mock shocked; then he runs downstage. He makes to speak, but the music grabs him, and he dances across the stage against his will. He crouches facing upstage, and Frank and Watson come on with palms in pots, dancing. They set them down, then exit. Brutus rushes to each of the plants and makes rebuking gestures. Then he goes to Wanda again, who's still undulating. He becomes mesmerized by her movements until she puts a foot on his shoulder and shoves him down. He scuttles away and climbs a ladder to sit on top of a pile of his possessions heaped in a corner, Right. As Frank and Watson reenter with more palms, dancing. They put these down also. Then Frank climbs a centrally placed ladder, and Watson stands on a box, upstage. He has a club. Wanda comes down, throws the big breaker switch, photoflash, and the loft lights bump up with tons of natural and electric light. We're back in Brutus' loft. All of Brutus' stuff has been shoved into one corner, and Brutus glowers on top of the clutter. Wanda's side looks great. It's decorated with several green palm trees. Frank sits on top*

* See Special Note on Songs and Recordings on copyright page.

of a step ladder at the dividing line between Wanda's stuff and Brutus' stuff. He's still got on his tuxedo shirt, minus the tie, and over that, a safari jacket. Watson, in sunglasses, a Castro hat, khaki pants and an orange shirt, leans against wall with his club in hand.

FRANK. So here we are.

WATSON. All present.

WANDA. Yowsa.

BRUTUS. Yes, here we are! You know. You know. I was just thinking about something. I was just thinking about my childhood. *(Music. The theme from* Lawrence of Arabia *comes in, under.)* To be exact, I wasn't exactly thinking about my childhood, which was shit. I was thinking about my heritage. Which I saw in a movie once. The desert! An endless palace of sky. My domain. Riding my camel into infinity. Yip, yip! Night comes. We make camp. We talk in the great tent about philosophy, mathematics. The hypnotic flames of the campfire blackening and illuminating our eyes. Spontaneously, we compose poetry of great insight and organic beauty. That's what you can never understand. You can never understand what I have lost. You can never understand what it is to be … *(Leaps to the deck as the main musical theme explodes.)* A Jew German! *(He takes a triumphal walk around the space. Gives Watson a disrespectful gesture. Then he pulls his headdress taut. The music ends abruptly. He does a little dance, chanting.)*
The sand is soft
Don't need no mattress
I'm a nomad
I got no address! *(Wanda gently removes Brutus' headdress, crosses to his hatbox, and puts it away.)*

WANDA. You know what your problem is, Brutus? You have a tendency to believe your own publicity. When I got here, this place was godawful. Now it's green. I see a spot that needs a plant. Bear with me now. Doesn't that look great?

BRUTUS. Do you see what she's doing? She put that plant right in the middle of what's left of my half of the apartment!

FRANK. Wanda, can you speak to that?

WANDA. It's just temporary. A little buffer until we work things out.

BRUTUS. And when would that be? You keep saying that and you keep pushing my stuff in the corner.

FRANK. Well, that's where I come in, Brutus. I'm here to help you and her to come to an understanding.

WATSON. But you're going to consult me, right?

FRANK. Absolutely, Watson. You got the big stick?

WATSON. *(Raps it twice on the wall.)* Right here.

FRANK. Good man. I'm sure we won't need it. So what do you all want?

BRUTUS. I'll tell you exactly what I want. I want her out.

FRANK. Not gonna happen.

BRUTUS. Why not?

FRANK. Not fair to Wanda.

BRUTUS. What about me?

FRANK. You've gotta be reasonable.

BRUTUS. It's my apartment, I want her out. That's reasonable.

WATSON. Wanda needs a place to live.

BRUTUS. So what? I need a place to live. This is it. I don't like these plants. I don't like any of this. I want my stuff where it used to be.

WANDA. You mean, all over the place. Well, that's not going to happen. You lost that right when you attacked me.

BRUTUS. Who are you to say what rights I have and what rights I don't have?

WANDA. I'm the woman with the gun.

WATSON. Bang, bang.

BRUTUS. What happened to the rule of law?

WANDA. Oh, so now you're Atticus Finch?

FRANK. I'll apply the law once we hash out what's legal.

BRUTUS. Who's going to decide that?

FRANK. Me.

WATSON. The Law is a living thing.

BRUTUS. Either I should be armed or you should disarm! *(Brutus has advanced towards Wanda. Watson steps in and whacks Brutus in the stomach with his club.)*

WATSON. That's far enough! *(Brutus staggers back to his side.)*

FRANK. *(To Watson.)* Stand down.

BRUTUS. I want my stuff spread out nice the way it was!

WANDA. You mean like a slob. Then I wouldn't have anywhere that was clearly mine.

WATSON. That would be confusing.

WANDA. And anyway, I have more stuff and nicer stuff than you.

FRANK. Let's not be judgmental.

BRUTUS. That's because I'm poor.

FRANK. You need a job?

WANDA. I'd be poor, too, if I didn't work.

WATSON. Lazy. We don't like that.

BRUTUS. I can't work under these circumstances.

FRANK. I hear you.

WANDA. You're a bum.

FRANK. That's inflammatory.

WANDA. It's a fact. You used to be somebody, but for the last ten thousand weeks you just read what you've already written.

BRUTUS. That's because I can't function in this living situation.

WANDA. What are you talking about? You weren't working when I got here.

BRUTUS. But I was thinking about it!

WATSON. Sure you were.

WANDA. All you do is talk about the glory days and knock up ignorant girls.

WATSON. Overpopulation.

WANDA. You're a bum!

BRUTUS. Who are you to call me a bum?

WANDA. Who am I? I'm not a bum, that's who I am. I'm a productive member of society.

FRANK. Cheese and crackers.

BRUTUS. How can I be productive when I'm so angry? It's insane what you're doing here. This is my apartment! I was so happy before you came.

WANDA. What are you talking about? You were miserable.

BRUTUS. But I had hope! I had the hope of being happy. Now I have no hope.

WANDA. So hope! Who's stopping you. Hope your brains out for what I care.

BRUTUS. I can't hope in this atmosphere of hostility and aggression. The situation's unbearable. To begin with, the bathroom's on her side.

FRANK. Wanda, that does seem tough.

WANDA. All he has to do is ask.

FRANK. Brutus?

BRUTUS. Well, I have to go now.

WANDA. No problem. Come ahead.

WATSON. Full speed. *(Brutus crosses to the bathroom. She draws her gun and blocks the way.)*

WANDA. I just have to check you out. Arms up? *(Brutus puts his arms out. She frisks him. He complains to Frank.)*

BRUTUS. This is what I have to go through. This is my life.

WANDA. You brought it on yourself. Drop the pants. *(He turns away from her, drops his pants.)*

WATSON. Bloody hell, I'm not here!

WANDA. Spread 'em. *(He spreads the cheeks of his ass. She shines a flashlight in his ass. She's satisfied.)* Okay. Pull 'em up. You can go in. *(Brutus exits into the bathroom.)*

FRANK. Jesus Christ, girl. What are you kids doing? This is no way to live.

WANDA. You think I like it? But you don't know this guy. You wouldn't believe the stuff I've found in his ass.

FRANK. It seems to me that this kind of atmosphere can only lead to terrific hostility and misunderstanding.

WANDA. What do you suggest?

WATSON. You know what I think?

FRANK. Hold the thought, Watson. I'm very interested in what you think, but I'm busy right now. *(To her.)* For starters, maybe you could give him a little more room. He's gotta get buggy living in that little bit of a corner.

WANDA. You know, I would love to do that. But first, I want him to show that he's changed. I want him to demonstrate that he's capable of being a good roommate.

FRANK. How?

WANDA. I'd like him to suck my foot.

FRANK. Huh? What?

WATSON. What's that?

WANDA. I'd like him to open his mouth very wide, so I can stuff my foot in it, and then I'd like him to suck it.

WATSON. Yucko.

FRANK. Wanda, has it ever occurred to you that what you may be looking for here is Revenge?

WANDA. I'm not interested in Revenge.

FRANK. That because there's a certain negative history here, that you and Brutus may simply not like each other enough to live in the one apartment?

WANDA. He's free to go. *(Brutus comes out of the bathroom with a detonator in his hand, and wires going into his clothing.)*

BRUTUS. I'm not going anywhere. I was here when you got here, and I'll be here when you're gone.

WANDA. Are you wearing explosives? *(Brutus lifts his shirt to reveal dynamite stuffed in his pants.)*

BRUTUS. That's right! *(Frank and Watson flee from Brutus.)*

FRANK. Whoa, Matilda! Fire in the hole!

WATSON. It's the blitz!

BRUTUS. This is what I have to do to be taken seriously! You all think you can decide my life without me. You are mistaken. My future's mine.

WANDA. Did you flush? *(She exits to the bathroom.)*

BRUTUS. I demand exactly half the apartment! No, better. I demand that everything go back to way it was before she moved in here! No, better yet! I demand that things go back to way they were before I was born.

WATSON. That isn't the future you're talking about, mate. That's the past.

WANDA. *(O.S.)* Oh! What a pig! *(The sound of a flush. She comes flying out of the bathroom.)* Let me lay it out for you. You wanna live with me, you flush.

BRUTUS. I don't want to live with you.

WANDA. Fine. Go back to the old days, call it the future, just do it somewhere else.

BRUTUS. I'm not leaving.

WANDA. Good. Perfect. Then join your dead relatives you love so much, cash your chips, go ahead, hit the detonator.

BRUTUS. You don't fool me. *(Grabs her hand and tries to force her to push the detonator button. She's terrified.)* You don't want to die, do you? Do you? And that's why I'm stronger than you.

WANDA. You don't know me! You don't know me! How 'bout this? *(She grabs the big stick from Watson, and hits Brutus' arm and then shoulder. Brutus falls down. She hits him three more times on the ground.)* How does this feel, you sadistic bastard!

BRUTUS. Oh my God! Help! She's a criminal!

WANDA. You hate me. You attack me. I fight back. You cry Foul. *(Watson steps towards Brutus.)*

WATSON. But he didn't attack. *(Wanda forces Watson back with the stick.)*

WANDA. He's wearing explosives!

BRUTUS. Did you see that? She hit me! Do it again. Where's my camera? Did you see what she did to me?

FRANK. Easy, Wanda.

BRUTUS. You're the sadist!

WANDA. And MY PEOPLE were here before YOU!

FRANK. Hey there, Wanda, that stick's for defense!

WATSON. She's out of control. *(She tosses the stick to Watson.)*

WANDA. I don't need the stick. I'll beat the shit outta you right now! Come on!

FRANK. What a piece of ass!

WANDA. That's right! *(To Brutus.)* You wanna fuck me, Popeye?!

BRUTUS. I'll push this button.

WANDA. *(Taunting him, touching her nipples.)* Push my button!

BRUTUS. I've already made my goodbye video. I have the courage. *(Wanda goads him, clucking like a chicken.)*

FRANK. Wanda!

BRUTUS. I have the courage! *(Brutus has been fending them off with the threat of the detonator. Frank and Watson are on one side, and Wanda on the other. Wanda tears the detonator out of his hand when he's distracted, tosses it away, pulls her gun, and starts backing Brutus up. He climbs up on top of his stuff during this next.)*

WANDA. Courage? Courage is a virtue. When you say someone has courage, that's a compliment. We do not compliment people for exploiting social covenants like Freedom and Trust for the purposes of murder!

WATSON. I hope Susan Sontag isn't here.

BRUTUS. Freedom.

WANDA. That's right. Freedom. You can't stop it, you can't fight it, it won't be denied.

FRANK. That's right. As a concept, it's a hands-down winner. Freedom. That's the temple of gold.

BRUTUS. Is it? I've seen nothing to show that Freedom makes you virtuous. You're not virtuous. You're just fat. You applaud your own lack of definition while you stuff your face. You love your fat ass while your soul starves. While children starve. What are you willing to give anybody without looking for something in return? Nothing. And that's why I'm going to prevail over you. Because I value my soul over my flesh. Because I'm willing to die.

WANDA. Nihilistic little git.

WATSON. It takes courage to kill yourself.

WANDA. It takes courage to get up in the morning and do something with your life. It takes courage to have children and educate them. To make things that are of use. It takes courage to live.

WATSON. It takes money, too.

FRANK. Watson. *(Wanda mutters in grief and anxiety.)*

WANDA. *Cherchez la femme?* Where has she gone? No more!

FRANK. What's the matter, Wanda?

WANDA. Too late. Nothing. I'm tired. I've been dealing with him for a little too long. I need a break. *(She pulls out her tank and remote.)* I think I'll go for a ride. *(She sets the little tank going across the floor.)*

BRUTUS. Where are you going? What are you doing? What is that?

FRANK. That's twenty-five-wheel drive.

WATSON. One hundred yards the gallon, fully loaded, automatic transmission.

BRUTUS. Stay away from the place where I pray.

WANDA. What do you mean? Your daddy's hatbox?

BRUTUS. Don't. That's where my father made his piety.

WANDA. I'm sure my grandfather prayed there, too.

FRANK. I think Jesus ate dinner there.

WATSON. Lunch it was!

BRUTUS. That's where my father talked to God. It's my only certainty. That's where I try to talk to God.

WANDA. Maybe it's where Abraham talked to God.

BRUTUS. Please. Don't mention Abraham.

WATSON. Abraham.

FRANK. Honest Abe.

BRUTUS. Have some respect for something in my house.

WANDA. I have a thought I'd like to share with you. *(She drives the tank nearer and nearer to the hatbox.)* Abraham is Abraham is Abraham. And this is in my way. *(She suddenly kicks the hatbox, destroying it. With an animal cry of pain, Brutus rushes to the ruined thing, picks it up, and takes it to his area.)*

BRUTUS. Cruelty. Your idea of freedom is cruel. *(Wanda pulls a potted plant onto the spot.)*

WANDA. Now doesn't that look better?

BRUTUS. Did you see that? Did you see? She doesn't respect anything about my life. She doesn't respect what's important to me. She wants respect. I can't take any more! And I won't. Die! *(Brutus has put down the remains of the hatbox and picked up a knife. He rushes Wanda during this next, trying to stab her. Watson grabs the knife arm, stopping him.)*

WATSON. Now! Now! Give it up! *(Frank plucks the knife from Brutus' hand. And then leads him away during this next.)*

FRANK. Come now, Mister Man. Don't get so het up. Look at me. Do I get excited? Be like me. You'll feel better.

BRUTUS. I don't want to be like you!

FRANK. Lemme talk to you. Are you willing to talk?

BRUTUS. I'll talk to anybody who wants to talk. I'm a reasonable man. It's her!

WANDA. Hah! *(Frank has taken Brutus off a little from Wanda.)*

FRANK. Lemme try something out on you. You seem like a savvy guy. I had some real estate problems early on in my life and I settled 'em pretty good. I see how it is with the apartment here. Seems to me like what you need is a fresh start. A whole new thing. *(Frank puts his arm around Brutus' shoulder.)* How 'bout we put you on a nice big reservation, set you up with a first-class casino?

BRUTUS. What do I look like? Set her up on a reservation. Give her a casino. I'm not leaving this apartment, she is.

WANDA. I have a God-given right to be here.

FRANK. Now let's not drag Jesus into this.

BRUTUS. She wasn't talking about Jesus, you moronic ill-informed nouveau riche pig!

FRANK. Oh that's right. You guys believe in a vengeful god. But hey, we're all children of Abraham, right? That's some story. That's a fork-in-the-road story. God tells Abraham to sacrifice his son Isaac. But at the last minute God said "Abe, scuttle that idea. Human sacrifice, dammit, we're past that." I believe that was the beginning of the Jesus angle. Drop that eye-for-an-eye thing, move on. You know what? I'd like to think if Adolf Hitler was a Christian, he wouldn't a killed the Jews.

WANDA. Adolf Hitler was a Christian.

FRANK. I'd like to think, if Hitler was Born Again, there never woulda been a Pearl Harbor.

WATSON. The Japanese bombed Pearl Harbor.

BRUTUS. They were backed into it by passive aggressive actions on the part of the United States.

FRANK. Who told you that?

BRUTUS. I read history.

FRANK. Well, you musta had the book upside down there, buddy. The Japanese started World War Two all by themselves. And they got their ass kicked.

BRUTUS. The Japanese were manipulated. They were victims.

FRANK. They were goosesteppers on the move.

WATSON. What about Hiroshima?

FRANK. Sometimes I wonder where you're coming from, Watson.

BRUTUS. But what about Hiroshima, Mister Nice Man? How do you explain Hiroshima?

FRANK. It's funny how you guys love to remember Hiroshima, but you get all fuzzy about Pearl Harbor. You ever hear of cause and effect?

BRUTUS. Who put you in charge of history? One man's integrity is another man's sin. You push me into a corner and leave me no civilized response. But I tell you! I will not be the villain!

WANDA. You should've thought of that before you tied me up and came at me with a power tool!

BRUTUS. And I'd do it again! You know why? Because you're a Nazi!

WANDA. I'm a Nazi? I'm a German Jew!

BRUTUS. And I'm a Jew German!

FRANK. Now maybe you guys could help me here. What's the difference between a German Jew and a Jew German?

BRUTUS. You're not serious.

FRANK. I'm know I'm a dumbass not to know, but humor me.

WANDA. A Jew German is a German Jew who hates himself!

BRUTUS. No, a Jew German has faith!

WANDA. A German Jew has faith! I don't know what a Jew German has! He believes Mohammed rode to heaven on a white horse!

BRUTUS. She believes the front page of *New York Times*! Who's crazy?

WANDA. I am a member of the modern world!

BRUTUS. I'll tell you what you are. You are a creature of racial theory. You, the German Jew, were created by Adolf Hitler.

WANDA. Keep Hitler out of this.

BRUTUS. It can't be done. Hitler made you.

WANDA. Don't!

BRUTUS. You're every bigot's fantasy. "Put them on a boat and send them somewhere. Give them their own country."

WANDA. Shut up!

BRUTUS. When you kill me, you kill yourself. When you kill yourself, you kill me.

WANDA. As long as you end up dead.

BRUTUS. Look at yourself in your righteousness. What you've become.

FRANK. Well, you know what the problem is.

BRUTUS. No, tell us.

FRANK. We're all Jews. That's the crux. That's what you have to understand. It's just that some of us is Jews with a twist is all.

WATSON. I'm Church of England.

FRANK. That's a Catholic with a twist. Catholic is a Jew with a twist. See what I'm saying? Muslim? You ever look at the Koran? The Koran is the Bible thrown in a blender. Muslim is a Jew with a twist. Me, I'm Born Again. But you know damn well what I was born first time. A Jew. We're all Jew boys here, squabblin' over who's got the best book. *(Points to Wanda.)* And this here's Mamma. That's Jew Mamma.

BRUTUS. That's not my Mamma.

FRANK. That's Jew Mamma.

BRUTUS. That's not my Mamma.

WANDA. If I was your Mamma, I'd slap my own face for what I done.

FRANK. All right, all right. People. How we gonna resolve this?

WATSON. Do you want my opinion?

FRANK. Sure, Watson, what is it?

WATSON. Well, I think you should be very cautious, that's all. Exercise restraint. This is a tricky situation and you wouldn't want to get it wrong.

FRANK. Thank you for that illumination. Look. I wanna get home tonight. I tell you what I'll do. I'll pay for a couple of Polacks to come down here and partition this place. That way you can share the apartment and not have to deal with each other. How's that?

BRUTUS. No.

WANDA. No. *(Wanda exits.)*

BRUTUS. Give me guns. Give me guns like you give her.

FRANK. No.

BRUTUS. Why not?

FRANK. Because, at your best, what you want doesn't exist. And at your worst, you're a genocidal street-hustling criminal fucker.

BRUTUS. I see I'm going to have to speak your language. What are you gonna do when you get home, Frank? Are you gonna cook? Will you be using any OIL? My family's kinda horrified at the way Wanda's been treating me.

FRANK. I have always had the greatest respect for your family.

BRUTUS. They'd like to see that reflected in the way you handle my apartment problem. *(Wanda reenters with some beautiful fabric and a candle. She crosses to downstage right. During this next, she kneels down, puts the fabric on, shawl-fashion, and lights the candle.)*

WANDA. You're a thug. That's what this is all about. You're a bum and a thug. I've dealt with thugs before. I tried to get along with them. It doesn't work. And I swore then. Never again.

FRANK. I like your grit, Wanda. But the danger with the show-down mentality is you end up in the middle of Main Street with fatalities.

WATSON. That's never stopped you.

FRANK. Watson there, you are a prickly pear.

WATSON. Sorry. *(Wanda, afflicted with anxiety and grief, mutters and rocks.)*

WANDA. *Cherchez la femme?* Where has she gone? No more.

FRANK. What's the matter, Wanda?

WANDA. Too late. You were right, Brutus. Fiction is dead. We see through the story. The fiction of civilization is dead. All that's left is the Beast.

BRUTUS. Are you calling me a Beast?

WANDA. Yes.

WATSON. It's her, Frank. She gives me pause, that's all. Who's to say she's not a little bit deluded? You know, I read a pamphlet a fella gave to me. It explains how there was no Holocaust.

BRUTUS. There's excellent good scholarship and pamphlets and websites that prove there wasn't. No Holocaust. Everything you do, you justify with this Holocaust, and maybe there was no Holocaust.

WANDA. Oh. Wouldn't you like to think so. Because if there was no Holocaust, then I never needed to come here in the first place. If there was no Holocaust, then I am the Holocaust.

BRUTUS. Maybe you are. Maybe you're a cancer! It's not right that you're here.

WANDA. But is it wrong? My friends, I have to be somewhere.

BRUTUS. So do I.

WANDA. I will be somewhere.

BRUTUS. So will I.

WANDA. I'm not going to vanish so that you don't have to feel guilty.

FRANK. Nobody's asking you to vanish.

WANDA. You're not, but they are.

WATSON. Maybe Frank doesn't have all the facts. Maybe if Frank had all the facts, he wouldn't side with you. He'd side with Brutus here.

FRANK. I'm not siding with anybody.

BRUTUS. That's a crock!

WANDA. You raped me. Every chance you got.

BRUTUS. You asked for it!

WANDA. How?

BRUTUS. You moved in here! What did you expect?

WANDA. I have to be somewhere. Does that mean I have to be raped?

64

BRUTUS. I'd do it again. *(She stands and asks, not without tenderness.)*
WANDA. What happened to you? You were a sophisticated man.
(Brutus starts to break down.)
BRUTUS. What good did it do me? I feel as if God cannot hear me. I pray and pray ... *(Wanda kneels down again.)*
WATSON. Maybe God doesn't like what you're doing.
BRUTUS. Shut your fucking mouth! What am I doing? Nothing but fighting back against years of humiliation at the hands of ... of ...
WANDA. God.
BRUTUS. No! God loves me.
WANDA. Why? Why would He love you?
BRUTUS. Because I am devout.
WANDA. I'm devout. Isn't God behind everything that happens? If you're unhappy with how life has treated you, isn't your argument with God and not with me?
BRUTUS. I have no quarrel with God.
WANDA. I think you do.
BRUTUS. I am in a fight to the death with a squatter.
WANDA. We're all squatters.
BRUTUS. I live here. I've always lived here.
WANDA. We're all refugees, we're all somebody's idea of scum. If History were about Justice, we'd all be on the street. Nobody's entitled to a home and we all need one.
WATSON. Now wait a minute. That's all well and true here, where there's nothing, but it's different with me. I have a culture. And culture deserves protection.
FRANK. Get off it, Boy! Don't get upright on me! You flushed some poor bastards out of their hole to make a place for yourself just like we all did. And you gotta live with that, just like we all do. But I am not going to stand here and allow the crimes of my grandfather, or the arrogance of your grandfather, or the lease of her grandfather, or the humiliation of his grandfather to stand in the way of a functioning civilization now! And I am by God gonna have that nice olive oil on my salad until I find something better!
BRUTUS. We'll see about that.
FRANK. Yes, sir. We shall.
WATSON. You're a bit selfish, Frank. And I don't feel completely consulted.

FRANK. You had your chance to rule the world, Watson. Did you do any better?

WATSON. No. But I'd like another shot.

BRUTUS. What about me? When do I get my turn?

FRANK. I ain't keep time to the tappin' toe of no ayatollah.

WATSON. I remember my past with a blushing lust.

WANDA. I remember when the world turned away and I was on fire.

BRUTUS. I will not endure my humiliation in peace! I remember when all of this was mine!

FRANK. I wish the lot of you would get amnesia! What good is history if all it does is drive you mad? What good is history if it's just a story that makes you hate?

WATSON. But but goddammit, man! Goddammit, Frank! If I am in some sense your father. If you are in some sense my son. Listen to me! You have no moral authority as long as you make and sell so many guns! So many guns. So many guns. *(Watson has been pulling guns out of Frank's pockets and throwing them on the floor. Watson walks away. Frank just stands there. A long pause.)*

FRANK. I don't like to think about that.

WATSON. You're not a simple man. You have to stop behaving as if you were a simple man. As if things were simple.

BRUTUS. No one's talking to me! No one's talking to me! Do you think I am an extension of your imagination? You take what's mine and you give it away. You give away my home. Why should I stand for it? I suffer! I am suffering!

WANDA. You want to know the truth? I know what's happening to you is wrong, and I don't care. You're the same animal that's always been chasing me. Well, I've stopped running, I've stopped dreaming of getting along with you. You can get along with me, you can leave, or you can drop dead. It's up to you.

BRUTUS. And do you think God likes what you're doing? Do you think God likes what you've become? *(Wanda stands up. She puts on her red beret. She turns to steel.)*

WANDA. It's my turn.

WATSON. To what?

BRUTUS. I don't have to put up with this. *(Brutus picks a gun off the floor.)*

FRANK. Watch out!

BRUTUS. No more. It ends now. Die! *(Music. The theme from Z or Zorba or some movie like that.* Brutus shoots her. The gun is fake, the gunshot prerecorded. She screams, but does not fall.)*

WANDA. OH NO YOU DON'T! NOT THIS TIME! *(She pulls her pistol and shoots him. Same deal. He cries out but does not fall. They stagger towards each other.)*

BRUTUS. I EXIST!

WANDA. I exist.

BRUTUS. GOD IS GREAT!

WANDA. God IS great!

BRUTUS. You ruined my life!

WANDA. If I die, you die! *(Wanda swings in slow motion, round-housing Brutus. They both cry "Boom!" to simulate the blow. Brutus swings at Wanda. Same deal. Then Wanda chokes Brutus and he makes a choking sound. Brutus now reciprocates. Same deal. Suddenly, they start making out, on the verge of fucking. They stop, just as suddenly, look at each other, and double over, making vomiting sounds. Then they stagger away from each other three steps, wipe their mouths, sigh in satisfaction, and look at Frank. Frank shakes his head.)*

FRANK. You two are some sick puppies. That was like watching a snake swallow its ass. *(He heads over to the pile of clutter, pulls out a card table that's folded up. He brings it Down Center, and starts snapping open the legs. The others all seem to have expected this, and start pulling up chairs.)* Shit. Anybody for a game of poker? I was hoping it wouldn't come to this, but you know how that goes. Last game I played lasted forty-five years or so. Hate to start another one so soon. Who's in? *(One by one they sit down at the table. One seat downstage is empty.)*

WATSON. I'll play. Tanks okay?

FRANK. Fine. Guns good with you?

WATSON. Why not.

WANDA. Deal me in.

BRUTUS. Can't we play chess?

FRANK. No. We got players to accommodate.

BRUTUS. All right.

FRANK. The old familiar faces.

WATSON. What are the stakes?

FRANK. We'll get to that.

BRUTUS. Frank?

FRANK. What?

BRUTUS. Would you mind if I called you something besides Frank?

FRANK. Like what?

BRUTUS. Would you mind if I called you Caesar?

FRANK. All right, you can call me Caesar, Brutus.

BRUTUS. I want the deal.

WANDA. No, me.

FRANK. Don't worry. Everybody's gonna have to deal.

WATSON. What are the stakes? *(Wanda is seized by emotion again, mutters.)*

WANDA. *Cherchez la femme?* Where has she gone? No more.

FRANK. What's the matter, Wanda?

WANDA. I'm pregnant. *(They gasp.)* Or am I dying?

FRANK. Those are the stakes.

WANDA. *(To the audience.)* Come and see us again.

BRUTUS. We're here every night.

WANDA. It's never exactly the same. But we're here.

FRANK. There's a seat here for ya.

BRUTUS. After all, we're playing with your money.

WANDA. And my life. *(Frank starts singing.)*

FRANK. CAMP TOWN RACES SING THIS SONG

WATSON. I'll take two.

FRANK. DO DAH! DO DAH!

BRUTUS. Two.

FRANK. CAMP TOWN RACE IS WAY TOO LONG

WANDA. One.

FRANK. ALL THE DO DAH DAY!

WATSON. Feeling lucky?

FRANK. GOIN' TO RUN ALL NIGHT!

WANDA and BRUTUS. Nah..

FRANK. GOIN' TO RUN ALL DAY …

WATSON. All together. *(Frank sings the verse again. And the others come in in a muted and sad way.)*

FRANK. CAMP TOWN RACES SING THIS SONG

OTHERS. DO DAH. DO DAH.

FRANK. CAMP TOWN RACE IS WAY TOO LONG
OTHERS. Yeah.
FRANK. ALL THE DO DAH DAY
OTHERS. GOIN' TO RUN ALL NIGHT
FRANK. GOIN' TO RUN ALL DAY
OTHERS. I BET MY MONEY ON THE BOB-TAILED NAG
FRANK. SOMEBODY BET ON THE GRAY
WATSON. Tragic, isn't it? *(The players lay down their cards and hold the pose. The light stays on them a long moment and then fades away.)*

End of Play

PROPERTY LIST

Coffee in a cardboard cup (BRUTUS)
Chess pieces (BRUTUS, LAWRENCE)
Walkman, headset (LAWRENCE)
Sign — "FICTION" (LAWRENCE)
Palm tree in luggage carrier (WANDA)
Valise, manuscript (BRUTUS)
Boxes for chess pieces (BRUTUS, LAWRENCE)
Two glasses of wine (BRUTUS, WANDA)
Table settings, vase with daisy, salad, olive oil
Studio light (BRUTUS)
Sawhorse, lumber (BRUTUS)
Hatbox (BRUTUS)
Bottle of whiskey, shot glasses (BRUTUS, FRANK, WATSON)
Blond wig, styrofoam head (BRUTUS)
White dress (BRUTUS)
Hat (BRUTUS)
Camera (BRUTUS)
Two ladders (BRUTUS, FRANK)
Rope (BRUTUS)
Gag (BRUTUS)
Goggles, circular saw (BRUTUS)
Candelabra (BRUTUS)
Nipple clips (BRUTUS)
Stereo remote control (BRUTUS)
Handkerchief (BRUTUS)
Sledgehammer (FRANK)
Guns (FRANK)
Playing cards (FRANK)
Sign — "NONFICTION" (WATSON)
Broom (WATSON)
Pack of cigarettes (FRANK)
Pill bottle, pills (FRANK)
Lemon slices (WATSON)
Piece of paper (WANDA)
Case of Coke, four six-packs (WATSON)
Toy tank with remote control (FRANK)

Arab headdress (BRUTUS)
Video camera (BRUTUS)
Microphones (WATSON, FRANK)
Gun in holster (WANDA)
Palm trees in pots (FRANK, WATSON)
Box (WATSON)
Club (WATSON)
Plants (WANDA)
Flashlight (WANDA)
Detonator, wires, dynamite (BRUTUS)
Knife (BRUTUS)
Fabric, candle (WANDA)
Card table (FRANK)

SOUND EFFECTS

Street sounds
Truck rumbling
Train approaching, train whistle
Beethoven's "Moonlight Sonata"
Tank rumbling
Arabian music
English backbenchers booing
Record scratching, hard rock instrumental music
Toilet flushing
Gunshots